VERONICA McGIVNEY

Motivating Unemployed Adults to Undertake Education and Training
Some British and Other European Findings

National Institute of Adult Continuing Education

*First published in 1992 by the National
Institute of Adult Continuing Education
(England and Wales)
19B De Montfort Street, Leicester LE1 7GE.*

© NIACE 1992

*All rights reserved. No reproduction, copy or
transmission of this publication may be made
without the written permission of the
publisher, save in accordance with the
provisions of the Copyright, Designs and
Patents Act 1988, or under the terms of any
licence permitting limited copying issued by
the Copyright Licensing Agency.*

British Library Cataloguing in Publication Data
*A CIP record for this book is available from
the British Library*

ISBN 1 872941 17 6

*Cover design Paul Vann
Data conversion and filmsetting
by Communitype, Leicester
Printed and bound in Great Britain
by Billing & Sons Ltd, Worcester*

Contents

Introduction v

Section 1
Explaining Lack of Motivation 1

Section 2
European Responses to Unemployment 12

Section 3
Effective Initiatives 30

Section 4
Factors Which Encourage Participation 48

Section 5
Conclusions 59

Bibliography 67

Author's Note

The NIACE REPLAN Motivation project was conducted in six weeks between April and August 1991. The report considers and summarises some of the issues involved in motivating unemployed people aged over 18 without skills and qualifications to participate in education and training programmes as a means of improving their position in the labour market. It draws on project and research reports and overviews from the UK and other EC countries to identify the reasons for low take-up of training programmes; the kind of programmes most likely to attract unqualified and low-skilled unemployed groups; and the factors which are most important in encouraging unemployed individuals to undertake education or training.

Acknowledgements

Many thanks are due to those who kindly provided the source documentation listed in the bibliography, and particularly to Sue Wood and David Parsons, Institute of Personnel Management; Peter Clyne, NIACE; Russell Gibbon, People and Work Unit; Monique Pincon-Charlot, Centre de Sociologie Urbaine, Paris; and Arlette Charlot, Tutor on RMI.

Note on references: Specific references, citations and sources are given in the text in the form of numbered notes, with a reference list at the end of each section. Where an author/date reference is given, details will be found in the bibliography.

Introduction

A Council of Europe report published in 1988 warned that massive unemployment, characterised by drop in demand for unskilled workers and growth of long-term unemployment, was likely to continue throughout Europe during the 1990s (1). This gloomy forecast is already being confirmed in the UK, where the decline in job opportunities in the manufacturing sector, the growth of service industries and the introduction of modern technology have combined to produce a situation in which less skilled work is fast diminishing (2). At the same time, insecure, short-term employment is increasing and it has become standard practice among the larger organisations and firms to employ around a small core of permanent workers 'a large periphery of temporary workers on "hire and fire" and short-term contracts – agency temps, outsources, self-employed and sub-contractors, that can be expanded or contracted according to demand' (3).

As unemployment grows, skilled and qualified workers are applying for unskilled jobs and unqualified school-leavers and unskilled workers are losing out in the competition for work. The competition for jobs has been described as a queue which qualified people and those with an uninterrupted work record can move up relatively quickly, leaving the rapidly growing numbers at the back unable to make any progress:

'As new people are constantly joining the queue, those at the back are prevented from moving up and become a hard core whose characteristics become increasingly intractable' (4).

A large number of those at the back of the queue are early school-leavers and people without qualifications. These now constitute a high proportion of the long-term unemployed, with some groups particularly vulnerable: people with literacy problems; older workers; people with physical or mental disabilities; ethnic minorities; and, increasingly on the continent of Europe, women (5).

Once out of work for a prolonged period, individuals accumulate additional handicaps: lacking both qualifications and recent work experience, they are progressively less able to meet rapidly changing skill needs and labour market demand. A survey into job vacancies in The Netherlands in the late 1980s showed that two out of three required not only general and specific work experience but also *recent* work experience, a situation typical of many European countries (6).

Since many long-term unemployed people lack the skills, qualifications and experience to match labour market requirements, the obvious solution would seem to be the provision of appropriate education and training schemes to help them make the transition back into paid work. However, a significant proportion of those eligible for places on British training schemes for the long-term unemployed either fail to take up places or drop out early from programmes. An estimate from the main referral routes suggests that for every 100 clients referred from Employment Services to the Employment Training (ET) scheme, 50 agree action plans with Training Agents and 40 start with Training Managers (7). The national picture is confirmed at local and regional levels. A project for the long-term unemployed in Gwent indicated that participation in Employment Training (ET) or Job Clubs was accorded lowest priority in participants' job-search efforts (8).

The White Paper *Training for Employment* describes lack of skills to fill the jobs available and lack of motivation to take up a job, training or other opportunities as 'major problems' which need to be tackled in order to get more unemployed people back into employment (Department of Employment, 1988). However, the assumption that prolonged unemployment is partly attributable to individual lack of motivation to undertake training or education needs to be examined.

There is, nevertheless, considerable evidence from both national and local surveys that those who left school at the earliest opportunity, the unqualified and the low skilled, are the people least likely to participate in any form of post-compulsory education and training. This applies whether they are in or out of work. A survey of adult participation in education and training in Scotland confirmed other large-scale surveys in its finding that far

Introduction

more people with qualifications express an interest in learning than those without (Munn and MacDonald, 1988). A survey of workers' attitudes to training in a variety of industrial contexts showed that unskilled and semi-skilled workers, and two subgroups within these categories – older workers and women – are strongly resistant to the idea of training (Fuller and Saunders, 1990a). Staff at a career service in the west of England are consulted by 'very few adults without qualifications' (9). Similar findings have been reported in many other parts of the world (10).

To ascribe such a widespread phenomenon to individual lack of motivation may be too simplistic. The following sections use reported experience and views from the UK and other parts of Europe to explore the concept of motivation in relation to education and training schemes for the unemployed. The sections attempt to answer some key questions:

- what causes low participation among unemployed adults without qualifications or skills?
- what kind of schemes have been developed to assist the long-term unemployed in different parts of Europe and how are these currently evolving?
- what types of training or education programme have attracted unqualified unemployed adults?
- what factors encourage the participation of unqualified and unskilled unemployed individuals in training and education programmes?

In such a short project, it was possible only to identify general trends and issues and what appear to be key 'motivational' factors. However, an important point to emerge from the available evidence is that the readiness and ability of unqualified and low skilled individuals to undertake training or education programmes are affected by a powerful combination of factors and disincentives, among which the prevailing employment situation, the extent and nature of the schemes available, the way they are presented and the rules governing benefit entitlement appear to play a crucial role. The evidence also shows that schemes can attract unqualified and unskilled people if they are based on a realistic understanding of the problems, circumstances and needs of individuals and if they offer real benefits to offset the perceived risks and costs of participation.

References

(1) J. Engelhardt, 1988, *Education des Adultes et Mutations Sociales. Etude préliminaire sur l'education des adultes chômeurs de longue durée: relations entre l'apprentissage et le travail*, Council of Europe.

(2) Institute of Personnel Management, 1990, *A Positive Policy for Training and Development* (revised version).

(3) A. Church, 1987, 'Inner city decline and regeneration', in P. Brown and D.N. Ashton (eds), *Redundancy, Unemployment and Labour Markets*, Falmer Press, quoted in L. Saunders, op. cit.

(4) G. Bogard, 1990a, *Adult Education and Social Change: The long-term unemployed:*, 1989 Consolidated progress report, Council for Cultural Co-operation.

(5) See ibid. and *ERGO: Quarterly Newsletter of the European Community Programme to Combat Long-Term Unemployment*, 1, Summer 1989.

(6) European Bureau of Adult Education (EBAE), 1988, *Adult Education and the Long-Term Unemployed*, 2.

(7) M.H. Banks and J. Bryn Davies, 1990, *Motivation, Unemployment and Employment Department Programmes*, Research Paper 80, MRC/ESRC Social and Applied Psychology Unit, Department of Psychology, University of Sheffield.

(8) People and Work Unit, 1990, *Helping Ourselves Back to Work: Providing effective support to the long-term unemployed*, Final Report, Newport, Gwent.

(9) N. Saint, 1990, 'Who needs adult careers guidance? A survey at Exeter Careers Office conducted between August 1987 and June 1990', *Newscheck with Careers Service Bulletin*, volume 1, number 6, December 1990, pp 19–20.

(10) See V. McGivney, 1990, 'Participation and non-participation: a review of the literature', in *Education's for Other People: Access to education for non-participant adults*, NIACE, pp 10–31.

Section 1
Explaining Lack of Motivation

Fuller and Saunders (1990a) argue that take-up of training will not increase significantly until the reasons for people's resistance are better understood.

The Role of Attitudes and Perceptions

Existing studies suggest that the reasons for non-participation are a complex and interacting mix of external (material, situational) and internal (cultural, attitudinal, dispositional) factors. Lack of time and finance are the most frequently cited barriers to adult participation in post-compulsory education and training. However, research suggests that dispositional or psychological factors play a crucial and determining role (McGivney, 1990). It is well established that many people who left school at an early age without qualifications associate education with 'boredom, irrelevance and failure' (1). Subsequent work experience may provide little evidence that further education or training will be of value to them. In their survey of attitudes to training, Fuller and Saunders (1990a) found that unskilled workers did not see any connection between formal training and jobs such as labouring and cleaning, while semi-skilled workers did not see how it would help them improve their performance or gain promotion. The researchers conclude that one of the most important disincentives to train may be the 'uneven connection between training, qualifications and career progression' (2).

The Role of Socio-economic Status

Surveys in many parts of the world suggest that there is a strong correlation between socio-economic level and the propensity to take up education and training. This, according to one European commentator, is because motivation to participate 'depends on the collective perception of access to social position ... Education does not play an equal role in the strategies for social advancement of different social groups' (3). Certain groups exhibit a strong resistance to education because they perceive it as reflecting the values and aspirations of other social classes. According to the Reference Group theory outlined by Gooderham (1987), individuals identify with the social and cultural group to which they belong – a 'normative reference group'. People who engage in education or training usually belong to a normative reference group that is positively oriented to education and training. Those who belong to a reference group where education and training are not 'normal' or customary activities will be reluctant to participate. This observation has been supported by a number of studies. For example, following the closure of the Consett steeworks, only about 30% of the unskilled and semi-skilled workers eligible attended paid education and training courses. Their reluctance was attributed largely to psychological factors – fears, anxieties and lack of confidence – and a strong feeling that a return to education would be abnormal and degrading and they might be laughed at by fellow workers (FEU, 1985). Similar attitudes to training expressed in the workplace led Fuller and Saunders (1990a) to reflect on the culture of solidarity associated with working-class jobs: the beliefs, attitudes and informal practices binding a group of workers together which create strong workplace norms and peer group pressure towards conformity:

> 'We found that where this sort of tendency exists (e.g. unionised factories) a negative training culture can develop because to engage in training is tantamount to breaking ranks' (4).

This solidarity can be reinforced at times of mass redundancy when groups whose working experience has been confined to a single industry view attempts to persuade them to train in new sectors with suspicion. Such a reaction was observed during a time of mass redundancies in the steel and textile industries in northern France. Here special education and training schemes were strongly resisted not only because they were not part of traditional group norms but because workers were sceptical about the value of training in occupational areas that might also be wiped out at a future date. Rejection of training in new skills also represented a protest against the destruction of their previous way of life (de Montlibert, 1973).

The Role of Unemployment

The irony is that unemployment, which might be expected to act as a stimulus to seeking education/training, appears to act instead as a powerful deterrent. All the evidence suggests that people in work are far more likely than the jobless to participate in education and training (5). There are a number of reasons for this. First, there is not always a clear link between unemployment and lack of education and training. For example, major reasons for long-term unemployment have been identified as:

- lack of basic skills
- family commitments, in particular, caring for dependent relatives
- ageism (resistance to accepting older adults on training courses and in employment)
- health or disablement problems (Engelhardt, 1988; Munn and MacDonald, 1988; People and Work Unit, 1990).

Only the first of these factors is related to lack of education and therefore susceptible to an educational solution; the others require changes in social policy and employer attitudes.

Secondly, prolonged unemployment brings in its train a host of negative consequences which sap both energy and spirit. These have been discussed in a plethora of reports and need only be summarised here:

- progressive loss of confidence and self-esteem: a report on

pre-employment training (Crowley-Bainton and White, 1990) comments on the lack of confidence that leads many unemployed to self-select themselves out of the job application process because they think they stand no chance of being chosen
- deterioration of personal and social skills
- growing social isolation
- personal and family stress
- lack of money
- perceived inability to initiate or control future events.

The last of these factors is perhaps under-estimated. According to the French researcher Jacques Hedoux: 'to undertake training implies an ability to anticipate, implement and react to a desired or experienced social change'. However, the hard core of unemployed non-participants he identified were people with limited autonomy and ability to formulate plans for the future: older adults, married women under the control of their spouses, people without qualifications and with limited work experience (6). High unemployment levels over the last decade have further eroded such people's capacity to help themselves. A large proportion of Europe's long-term unemployed have, according to Engelhardt (1988), lost hope and belief in their capacity to change their situation. Engelhardt contends that the long-term unemployed now constitute a 'new social group': a non-working culture defined by lack of confidence, despair and defeatism. In a British study, Lindley (1991) observes that this psychological environment is not a good one in which to urge unemployed individuals to take the initiative and responsibility for their own training. He argues that what is perceived as lack of motivation stems from the different choices and constraints faced by different groups, their relative situations and circumstances and their existing experience of vocational education and training.

The Role of Recent Training Experience

Lindley has found that recent experience of training stimulates individuals to seek further training and that this phenomenon is most clearly visible in the case of workers over 45 – a group among whom readiness to participate in training or other forms of education is generally low. The same logic applies in reverse: lack of education and training experience tends to act as a demotivator. Therefore, to attract unemployed adults with no experience of post-school training or education, the options available need to offer very clear 'payoffs' in the form of financial allowances or increased job opportunities. There can be a problem, however, in proving that there is a clear connection between training and finding employment.

Lack of Perceived Links Between Training and Jobs or Career Progression

Data collected from a variety of industrial and commercial contexts convinced Fuller and Saunders (1990a) that a significant proportion of low-skilled and semi-skilled workers do not share the official enthusiasm for training because they do not see any connection between training and career progression. If those *with* jobs fail to see the connection, then it is not surprising that unemployed people are sceptical about the links between training and job prospects, particularly in times or areas of high unemployment. This applies particularly to older unemployed individuals in a culture where age is a considerable barrier to finding employment (People and Work Unit, 1987). Lindley (1991) argues that it is not lack of motivation that deters older unemployed adults from seeking training but external structures and pressures related to different stages in the working life-cycle: for example, the powerful institutional and financial incentives to take early retirement which undermine older individuals' willingness to train or seek career changes. This has a knock-on effect with younger workers, who are less likely to invest in training for what may be a comparatively short working life.

Young unemployed adults also experience disincentives to train. In her evaluation of the Docklands Skillnet programme, Lesley Saunders cites research which suggests that young unemployed adults' attitudes to training are largely influenced by the condition of the labour market:

> *'If employment levels deteriorate, attitudes towards training are likely to become more negative; if the job situation improves, then the demand for training from young adults is likely to increase'* (7).

White (1990) also points out how difficult it is for unemployed young adults without qualifications to obtain information about labour market opportunities, as they have limited or no experience of work and therefore little access to 'inside' information. He claims that what is interpreted as lack of motivation to find work is often due to ignorance about where to look for opportunities when most advertised jobs demand qualifications.

The Role of Individual Observation and Experience

Decisions to undertake training are therefore strongly influenced by what unemployed individuals observe to be happening around them. This can be at variance with the optimistic messages contained in advertisements and literature about special schemes. For example, if low-skilled, unqualified people are seen to be acquiring jobs without benefit of training, other unemployed people in this category will hope to do likewise (Church, 1987). Similarly, if they see that individuals who have taken training are not acquiring jobs, this will confirm that training has no value. Reports on the experience of long-term unemployed people who have participated in training schemes suggest that programmes often do not take sufficient account of clients' real chances in the labour market and raise hopes that may be subsequently dashed. For example, a survey of older long-term unemployed in Wales revealed that none of a sample from the coal and steel industries who had trained in new occupational areas had found employment. This engendered a view of training as an irrelevance and a time-filler (People and Work Unit, 1987). Not surprisingly, a later project in Wales found that front-line Employment Services staff were having increasing difficulty in persuading long-term unemployed individuals of the value of menu items. The project report comments on the frustration and disillusionment felt by those who attend RESTART interviews but then fail to be accepted on the ET programme and return to unemployment:

> 'Most [RESTART interviewees] become more hopeful the first time they attend, some even regaining something of their lost confidence and self-esteem. They are then returned in effect to their earlier hapless position, possibly the more disillusioned, even cynical about their experience and the future' (8).

Deficiencies in the Presentation of Education/training Schemes

In Britain there are sometimes problems at the interface between unemployed people and employment services which contribute to clients' lack of interest in the available options. For example, resistance to official schemes may be intensified if initial approaches, such as invitations to attend RESTART interviews, are brusque and officious (People and Work Unit, 1990), and if communications fail to convey adequate information and explanations of what the options are and what is expected of unemployed clients. There is considerable evidence that unemployed individuals with no post-school education or training experience are confused by the complexity of available options and do not always have a clear understanding of what participation in training schemes might involve (Banks and Bryn Davies, 1990). They are particularly confused by the regulations regarding benefit entitlement and the '21-hour rule' affecting decisions to study, which varies according to the type of benefit claimed and is affected by the 1989 Social Security Act requirement that unemployment benefit claimants must provide regular proof that they are 'actively seeking work'.

Lack of liaison between education providers, employment services and social security offices means that potential students sometimes receive inadequate or inaccurate information on their continuing eligibility to receive benefit, and this leads to misconceptions, uncertainty and anxiety. Reports indicate that unemployed people's anxieties are not always allayed by clear explanations and counselling. The consensus among Employment Services staff interviewed during the Welsh project (People and Work Unit, 1990) was that they they did not have the time, knowledge and skills to provide the long-term unemployed with the in-depth counselling they required. In their study of motivation in relation to Employment Department programmes, Banks and Bryn Davies (1990) found that 'mixed messages' and lack of clear information in the counselling process lead to worry, uncertainty and eventual drop-out from programmes. One of the results of inadequate information, guidance and counselling which they note is the spread of 'bad news' about national schemes. Banks and Bryn Davies report that negative hearsay is a major reason for non-participation, citing studies which reveal that in areas of high unemployment, government training schemes are widely perceived to be exploitative (providing employers with cheap and expendable labour) and ineffective in helping people to get permanent jobs. Until this image is dispelled, the difficulties of persuading unqualified long-term unemployed individuals to attend schemes voluntarily will persist.

The Perceived Risks of Participation

There is a broad consensus among researchers and education/training practitioners in Britain that the most powerful disincentive to train is the potential risk to benefit entitlement and a precarious financial stability:

> 'The view is, once you've got benefit sorted out, DON'T TOUCH IT, especially if the course is only for a few weeks' (9).

> 'Any potential changes constitute a threat to adapted regimes, renegotiated family roles and to security of income from benefits, however low' (10).

> 'People with low earning capacity may on paper be able to increase it by mixing benefits and low-waged employment or benefits and trainee wages or allowances, but the risks they perceive make

short-run imperatives take precedence. In the case of the training option, there may be the added uncertainty of whether or not the training will significantly increase pay and employability (11).

Lindley (1991) suggests that fears of putting a relatively stable benefit position at risk, together with the increasing difficulties in finding jobs and the greater insecurity of the jobs available, combine to 'immobilise' unemployed individuals. Even though trainees on the ET scheme receive £10 on top of benefits, this may be too low to act as a motivator for many unemployed people. Banks and Bryn Davies argue that 'having learned to exist in a rigid money management system, they have difficulty in absorbing additional marginal costs that are entailed in entering training.' They predict that until the issue of training allowances is addressed, certain groups of unemployed will not participate in schemes 'unless by coercion, in which case their psychological motivation will be well-nigh zero' (12).

The Barriers Faced by Specific Groups

The Welsh report on work with the long-term unemployed highlights the irony that clients who have attended RESTART interviews are more likely to experience disincentives than incentives to undertake training. The evidence shows that some groups are particularly disadvantaged. A number of surveys have found that black people face acute difficulties in gaining access to appropriate schemes and in finding work placements and jobs. Moreover, their participation in training schemes does nothing to change the racism and stereotyping many ethnic minority individuals encounter in the labour market (13). A tutor involved in government schemes in France reports that skin colour appears to play a decisive role in the difficulties faced by immigrant women in finding work placements to supplement their training (14). Unskilled and semi-skilled women also experience considerable barriers to participation in training and employment schemes: for example, limited time, domestic constraints, lack of childcare facilities and the cost of childcare (the ET programme takes account only of the childcare problems of single parents). Further deterrents have been identified as lack of self-confidence and low expectations and aspirations. Unskilled women, particularly those with family responsibilities, have access mainly to part-time, low-paid work with no progression or promotion prospects. Women in such jobs rarely have access to funded opportunities for training and education, even if they had the time to participate. Fuller and Saunders (1990a) comment on the tension between work operations and training and the fact that part-time or temporary workers have no time within work schedules to undertake training programmes.

There are, therefore, multiple reasons for low participation rates among low-skilled and unqualified groups, with the evidence cumulatively suggesting that the odds are heavily weighted against their involvement in training so long as the costs (in all senses of the word) exceed the potential returns. Given the range and complexity of the demotivating factors, it may be that too much is expected of people who have been out of work for long periods. One report on European programmes for the long-term unemployed makes the point that long-term unemployed people are in a paradoxical situation:

> 'They are expected to be more mobile, more intelligent, more determined, richer, etc. than most of the population of working age in searching for a job, spending money on newspapers, making telephone calls, writing letters and travelling about, with unfaltering motivation' (15).

Bogard (1990b) argues that the problem of low participation has less to do with individual motivation than with the processes, definitions and categories used in a structural exclusion process:

> 'The unemployed are not inherently motivated/unmotivated or employable/unemployable. These are results rather than causes of the exclusion process, of the categorisations used by the various social agencies (firms, employment services, social services, training and counselling services)' (16).

He refers to a process of conscious or unconscious discrimination in some European countries which influences course entry arrangements and the way unemployed target groups are defined. This implies that national training or education programmes for the unemployed and the way they are administered may, albeit unintentionally, undermine people's readiness or ability to participate. The grounds for this view are explored in the next section.

References

(1) Sir Christopher Ball, quoted in *Education*, 26 April 1991.
(2) A. Fuller and M. Saunders, 1990a, *The Potential Take-Up of Mass Training*, Institute for Research and Development in Post-Compulsory Education, Lancaster University, pp 5–6.
(3) G. Bogard, 1990a, op. cit., p 19.
(4) A. Fuller and M. Saunders, 1990a, op. cit., p 9
(5) See V. McGivney, 1990, op. cit., pp 10–30.
(6) J. Hedoux, 1981, 'Les non-publics de la formation collective', *Education Permanente*, number 61, pp 89–105.
(7) D.N. Ashton and M.J. Maguire, undated, *Young Adults in the Labour Market*, Department of Employment Research Paper No 55, University of Leicester, quoted in L. Saunders, 1989, op. cit., p 26.
(8) People and Work Unit, op. cit., pp 27–28.
(9) Tutor on course for the unemployed quoted in V. McGivney, 1990, op. cit., p 89.
(10) People and Work Unit, 1990, op. cit., pp 31–32, 90.
(11) R.M. Lindley, 1991, 'Individuals, human resources and markets', in J. Stevens and R. Mackay (eds), *Training and Competetiveness*, NEDO Policy Issues Series, Kogan Page, pp 210–211, 217.
(12) M.H. Banks and J. Bryn Davies, 1990, op. cit., paras S7 and S15.
(13) See V. McGivney, 1990, op. cit., pp 105–112.
(14) A. Charlot, 1991, in correspondence with author.
(15) G. Bogard, 1990a, op. cit., p 9.
(16) G. Bogard, 1990b, *Adult Education and Social Change: The long-term unemployed*, 1989 Consolidated Progress Report, Council for Cultural Co-operation, Strasbourg, p 20.

Section 2

European Responses To Unemployment

Unemployed people's motivation to participate in education and training schemes cannot be considered in isolation from the changing employment situation and the nature of the different programmes on offer.

Reports on European schemes for the unemployed indicate that the stress in the EC as a whole has been on vocational education and training, with priority given to training programmes in the sectors and regions most hit by recession. Since the mid-1970s, the typical European response to increasing long-term unemployment has been to transfer public finance from adult education to training geared to the labour market, usually involving a placement element. Although this strategy has helped many individuals and progress has been made in bringing industry and training providers together, it has not had the desired outcome of getting the most disadvantaged long-term unemployed back into the labour market. For example, the city of Nurnberg spent five million DM over a five-year period on temporary employment and placement measures 'to no effect whatsoever' (Bogard, 1990b). Similarly, a common criticism of the Employment Training (ET) programme, currently the main option for the unemployed in England and Wales, is that only a small proportion of trainees subsequently find work or acquire a qualification (1).

Recent overviews of national schemes for the unemployed have highlighted the following major problems:

- insufficient places
- inappropriate training responses
- insufficient help for the most disadvantaged
- discriminatory selection procedures

- separation between education sectors.

Each of these is now considered in turn.

Insufficient Places

A recurrent criticism is that national training strategies have not kept pace with the growing numbers of long-term unemployed. Estimates of the proportion of long-term unemployed people participating in education, training and other measures in EC member states in 1986 (the latest year for which such estimates could be compiled) reveal that in all countries except Belgium fewer than 50% of those eligible participated in any special measure. This was ascribed partly to the fact that national education and training measures were 'conspicuously limited' in all the countries covered except France, and even there provision did not extend to two-thirds of the long-term unemployed. The analysts conclude from this that participation rates may be related more to the amount of finance allocated to unemployment measures than to individual motivation (2).

The experience of individual countries lends support to this view. In England and Wales, for example, despite the recent growth in unemployment, the training budgets available to the Training and Enterprise Councils, which are now responsible for delivering programmes for the unemployed, have been reduced (3). This has led observers to suggest that the real issue is not how the unemployed can be motivated to participate in training but how policy-makers can be motivated to set up an adequate and coherent framework of education and training for the unemployed:

> 'The infrastructure is wrong. Training here is characterised by stop-go, inconsistency and gaps. Conflicts about the costs of training and who will bear them have resulted in an inadequate number of under-resourced programmes' (Education and Training Manager, Institute of Personnel Management).

Inappropriate Training Responses

In many countries, the tendency has been to develop training schemes in response to economic needs and official views of what unemployed people require in order to return to the labour market. The problem with this is that the education and training needs identified by government may not be those recognised by unemployed people themselves and thus may have no motivational effect. The gap between providers and potential client groups is further widened when, as reported by Saunders (1989), training schemes for the unemployed are designed not in response to their expressed needs but according to external factors and criteria such as participating institutions' administrative procedures, staffing and curricular capacity. This seems to be a common feature of national programmes for the unemployed. In Canada, for example, Edwards (1991) found that unemployed people were allocated to training programmes on the basis of bureaucratic criteria rather than their particular requirements or interests.

There seems, therefore, to be a tendency in national schemes to provide a blanket response to jobless people without regard for the specific circumstances, experience, learning barriers and needs of individuals, and without a realistic appraisal of their chances in the current labour market. This can be clearly seen in relation to unemployed women. Eight years of running courses for unemployed women in Berlin has led one adult education organiser to express her frustration at the inappropriateness of both the approach and the content:

> 'Tutors were being asked to motivate women who were already highly motivated; to give time management skills to women who had for years been running households and rearing children as well as undertaking paid work; to help women get qualifications and teach them how to apply for jobs, when there were only low status, low paid jobs available' (4).

Another report on vocational training for women in Europe questions the practice of providing the same training programmes for both sexes:

European Responses to Unemployment

'Programmes which offer equal access in theory, without making provision for women to overcome their barriers, are unlikely to achieve any practical improvement in participation' (5).

Insufficient Help for the Most Disadvantaged Unemployed Groups

There is a growing view among educationists in Europe that narrow, labour market-linked education/training is not the right solution to long-term unemployment. Engelhardt (1988) describes it as the solution of the 1950s and 1960s to short-term unemployment and argues that different measures are required to solve long-term unemployment. Like many other commentators he claims that narrow, specialised occupational training is inappropriate for people with disadvantages such as illiteracy, lack of confidence and absence of working experience. From their overviews of education/training schemes for the long-term unemployed across Europe, both Engelhardt and Bogard conclude that adults with limited initial schooling and no qualifications need preparatory or induction courses before they can fully participate in training. But, according to Bogard (1990b), training providers implementing national schemes are generally inexperienced in working with such groups. This is borne out in an evaluation of the ET programme in England and Wales:

'There is insufficient time and expertise to provide the initial assessment and guidance for those requiring help with basic skills, language or special needs, a lack of a single identifiable source of guidance and counselling and difficulty in finding suitable placements' (6).

Discriminatory Selection Procedures

There are also signs that some individuals with preparatory or remedial learning needs are being denied access to national training schemes through a selection process which occurs within a preliminary guidance or orientation interview. Bogard (1990b) reports that selection processes are applied at the start of some European training programmes, with the result that individuals needing preparatory or remedial work are passed over in favour of those considered to have sufficient potential to produce the desired outcomes. The same point has been made by Saunders (1989), who, during her evaluation of the Skillnet Quick Start initiative, found some training agencies operating an initial selection process to screen out candidates perceived as less employable. In this way, training schemes for the unemployed paradoxically reflect and perpetuate the labour market selection processes which make people unemployed in the first place. This is a logical result of schemes which seek simultaneously to achieve greater employability and to comply with employer demand. Council of Europe reports on education and training programmes for the long-term unemployed refer to employers' attempts to minimise risks by avoiding people with visible disadvantages and long unemployment records. For example, negotiators at employment exchanges in Belgium are 'market conscious' and reject social security claimants in order to comply with employers' wishes to avoid 'social misfits' (Bogard, 1990b).

It has been suggested that participation in special training schemes reduces rather than increases a person's 'employability'. A study of a sample of trainees in the former Youth Opportunities Programme revealed a link between participation and diminishing employment prospects, even after qualifications were taken into account (White, 1990). This paradox was ascribed to the fact that the six months' placement could be seen as an extended selection process, at the end of which those trainees retained by employers would be perceived as successful workers, while those not retained would be considered failures. In the case of the latter, participation in the scheme would send a 'negative signal' to potential employers. White's subsequent argument could apply to all employment training schemes: the more effective such programmes are with some individuals, the more they harm the prospects of others. People who have not been admitted to a programme in the first place may be perceived as not worth the trouble of training, while those who are accepted but who do not subsequently find a job may be seen as not capable of benefiting from a special programme. Moreover, the mere fact that an individual has been on a programme designed for the long-term unemployed can in itself represent a 'negative signal' for employers. White therefore argues for schemes for the unemployed to be 'invisible', i.e. indistinguishable from training schemes for employed people.

Separation Between Education Sectors

More than a decade of high unemployment has led to the emergence of an argument for greater integration of the education sectors in providing schemes to help the long-term unemployed. In many European countries, the structures and organisation of occupational training and adult education in a wider sense are separated. This has led to limited links and co-operation between adult education providers and those responsible for labour market training. There is now a widespread view in Europe that this separation is damaging (7). Speaking at the Third European Congress on Continuing Education and Training in 1991, the EC Commissioner for Employment, Industrial Relations and Social Affairs, Mrs Papandreou, deplored the 'artificial and damaging gap' maintained in Europe between education and training:

> 'EC member states have not yet succeeded in bridging the gap between continuing training for the highly qualified workers who are already aware of the benefits of such an investment and who offer a quick "return" for companies, and the others – those unskilled workers and the unemployed who, on the whole, are left over to the State ... this trend may contribute to even greater social and economic segregation' (8).

Unemployed people themselves may help to reinforce the distinction. Projects in Scandinavian countries between 1985 and 1987 revealed 'very traditional attitudes' among the long-term unemployed towards the nature and goals of learning. They were very suspicious of 'creative' work, preferring 'useful and necessary skills' (Engelhardt, 1988). Similarly, White (1989) reported that although one of the perceived problems with the YTS scheme was that it was too narrowly job-related, both employers and trainees have resisted the inclusion of transferable skills as both parties are concerned with the end results – finding a job or a suitable employee.

Engelhardt (1988) describes the separation of the education and training sectors as obsolete and argues the need for co-operation and integration to help people adjust to the profound economic, social and cultural changes currently taking place on a global scale. With the growth of unemployment, however, the gap between education and training seems to be widening rather than diminishing in some countries, and adult educationists from several parts of Europe complain that one of the results of recent policies has been to marginalise 'soft' (non-vocational) skills because they are not considered of economic value (9). In England and Wales, although the value of general education is now being recognised by employers, and although the Secretary of State for Employment has referred to the need for 'a much stronger base of general competences at all levels in the workforce' (10), unemployed people have to conform with an increasingly narrow and limiting perception of what is useful in employment-seeking terms. Moreover, current educational policy seems destined to drive an even greater wedge between 'general' and 'vocational' education. A national discussion paper refers to training programmes in Britain being 'trapped by unhelpful distinctions' between education and training and ignoring the skills and experience of adult educators in working with unqualified and less educated adult learners (11).

Current Strategies

The continuation of long-term unemployment is obliging some European governments to rethink their strategies. An EC report on combating long-term unemployment in EC member states since 1984 has concluded that the three necessary conditions for combating long-term unemployment are:

- reskilling
- fairer representation of the long-term unemployed in national training programmes
- some form of job guarantee after a period of reskilling and retraining.

Specific recommendations include:

Preventive measures

- one-to-one counselling at the onset of unemployment and regular personal contact thereafter to ensure people are fully acquainted with employment and training opportunities
- training which is specially geared to the needs of the local or national economy.

Reintegrative measures

- counselling
- reorientation projects to build self-confidence, motivation for education or training and job-search techniques
- vocational education or training towards recognised qualifications (e.g. the modular training system in France and the 'Building on Experience' scheme in Ireland) (12).

These recommendations reflect the general direction unemployment initiatives are currently taking in a number of European countries. A CEDEFOP report (1990) observes that despite the institutional pluralism in different EC member states, common approaches to problem-solving can be detected, notably: 'a growing attention to providing services featuring interaction and co-ordination of guidance, training and employment' (13). An example of this approach can be found in France, where the results of various national measures for the long-term unemployed during the 1980s have convinced policy-makers of the need for:

- personal guidance, counselling and diagnosis
- comprehensive strategies involving training and support measures to help people seek work
- additional social measures alongside and within training to help remotivate people and rebuild their confidence.

These conclusions led the French Government in 1989 to adopt Le Plan pour L'Emploi – a comprehensive, better resourced scheme for the long-term unemployed involving certain changes of direction, namely:

1. Greater simplicity. As the plethora of previous schemes had caused confusion, a new state-funded training strategy – Les Actions d'Insertion et de Formation (AIF) – combining all programmes except one directed at 'isolated women' was introduced at the beginning of 1990.

2. Individualisation of training routes. Although the focus of training measures was still to be on qualifications, retraining, skills acquisition and updating, recognition of the diversity of unemployed people and their circumstances led to the conclusion that greater effectiveness would be gained through personalised routes into training. Training courses were to be more flexible and modularised, with individuals following a learning plan negotiated with providers beforehand.

3. Funding for regional programmes based on identified needs and priorities.

4. Expansion of target groups, with priority given to those most disadvantaged (14).

Guidance and Counselling

The importance of guidance and counselling for unemployed people, particularly those who are unskilled and unqualified, is widely accepted throughout Europe. The CEDEFOP (1990) study reports that group guidance is assuming increasing importance in European training schemes for the long-term unemployed and that trainers find groups provide valuable support for individuals and often motivate people to take self-help action. In some cases, group guidance and counselling involves useful visits to firms and meetings with employers. In Denmark, unemployed groups are offered two weeks of guidance sessions and 'inspiration courses' designed to improve self-confidence and strengthen support processes within the group. Sessions typically begin with a workshop at which participants share ideas and aspirations and discuss their training and work experience. The sessions include visits to firms and studying job application methods. In Spain, an association of adult training centres has set up a number of pilot projects in which co-ordinated guidance and training schemes are geared to local employment initiatives, particularly to the 'social economy' sector. In Bremen, local programmes for the unemployed combine pre-training measures, 'psycho-social stabilisation', information and advice and general occupational guidance. The Vocational Training Foundation in Hamburg provides a similar mix in its vocational training schemes for 'people unaccustomed to learning.' Long-term unemployed people are offered five weeks' assessment and guidance (15).

Individual guidance, particularly at the beginning of unemployment, is widely viewed as one of the most important processes in facilitating unemployed people's access to education and training (Engelhardt, 1988). Initial guidance therefore plays an important part in most European schemes. In The Netherlands, 'Fresh Start' guidance interviews are even conducted with unemployed people in their homes (although the danger that this approach may be seen as a form of monitoring is acknowledged). In Britain, national programmes for the unemployed are also preceded by a guidance, counselling and assessment period, although concern has been expressed that the process is sometimes confused by clients with the regulations and demands of the social security benefit system:

'RESTART interviews sometimes involve a confict between feeling coerced into action and genuinely deciding on the best choice from the menu of options. The counselling function and the administration of benefit become confused in the minds of clients' (16).

The Principal of an English further education college which attracts many unemployed people without qualifications or post-school education to a special 'Alternative Programme' claims that without initial guidance and counselling, such people would not come into the course. (17).

One of the most valuable roles of initial guidance is to help people recognise and evaluate their existing skills and experience. In France, participants on government training schemes have access to a service which helps them identify and evaluate the skills they have acquired during work and training as well as in their personal and social life ('bilan personnel et professionel'). By 1988, 30 Review Centres had been established, all based on close inter-agency and interdisciplinary co-operation. Specialists from different sectors and agencies co-operate in compiling as complete a list as possible of job seekers' personal and professional experience before helping them to draw up a 'vocational integration plan'.

Collaboration is also a feature of regional vocational guidance centres in The Netherlands, where there is co-operation between the local authorities, social services and employment offices in Fresh Start interviews. Similar local networks with emphasis on guidance and co-ordination of activities have been set up by Forderwerk in Bremen.

Individualised Training Plans

The principle of giving unemployed people the opportunity to discuss and plan their individual education or training routes is becoming widely accepted in Europe. For example, in England and Wales, individual action plans are an important part of the current national training programme in which:

> *'The emphasis on building an individual plan for each trainee clearly plays a valuable role in alerting all concerned – trainee, trainer and employer – to the individual's distinctive starting point and aspirations'* (18).

Individualised training strategies involve evaluation of individual experience, background and prior skills, negotiation of learning routes and regular assessment. Bogard (1990a) describes the process as an important step towards responsibility and personal autonomy. But he warns that if schemes are too narrowly conceived, they may undermine the negotiation process. For, while the principle of personalised training, in which participants have a determining role should make negotiation a key phase, the more a scheme is geared to finding a job, the more negotiation may be neglected and subordinated to the requirements of syllabus and performance. Bogard also argues that personalised training requires an appropriate information system enabling people to make more informed choices, and a more qualitative system of appraisal than selection interviews. He warns that it can be a complex and lengthy process to develop sustainable training plans with people who may have very traditional ideas about content and teaching methods, and who, after a long period of unemployment, have fallen into a pattern of dependency.

Pre-vocational Courses

Experience in Europe has shown that many people without qualifications and post-school education and training experience cannot be integrated directly into training programmes. They require forms of introductory education or training to help them acquire or re-establish basic skills and confidence, and to give them access to the basic competences they need in order to compete and function in the labour market. Women without qualifications who have spent time at home raising families often need women-only pre-training courses or tasters to re-establish confidence, basic skills and workplace skills.

In Denmark, preparatory courses lasting from several weeks to three or four months have been established to help unemployed adults return to education. Without this kind of preparation, some well-meaning initiatives fail. For example, a second chance learning scheme piloted in Ireland to enable unqualified long-term unemployed individuals to take a full-time leaving certificate course failed to recruit, leading to the observation:

> *'It is naive perhaps to think that unemployed people, many of whom are educationally damaged, will go straight into a leaving certificate course' (19).*

Towards a Broader Conception of Schemes

Since narrow labour market-linked approaches do not appear to have helped many of the low-skilled and unqualified unemployed, some analysts of the European scene have been calling for the development of a wider kind of education programme. It has been argued, for example, that while labour market skills – occupational skills, technical skills, specialist and theoretical knowledge – are useful, they do not protect the most long-term unemployed individuals from the vicissitudes of the economy: 'the employment market is a wider concept, to do with job seeking, knowing one's abilities, recognising opportunities and appreciating the need for retraining' (20).

Bogard argues that strategies to change long-term unemployed individuals into active and more independent participants in the life of the community require a broader approach which combines vocational education, academic education and the development of social skills. Another study of European schemes for the unemployed refers to:

> *'the growing realisation that unemployment has social and psychological effects requiring the development of provision which is on the borderland between education programmes, social work and psychological care'* (21).

This realisation is central to the adult education projects for the long-term unemployed in five European countries discussed by Bogard (1990a, b). These had both short-term and long-term aims: to provide a more effective response to the needs arising from hard core unemployment; to combat marginalisation and social isolation and to enable people to become more socially participative and more economically active. The author argues that these aims are complementary and that initiatives which address only only of the target group's needs – employment or social integration – fail by 'reinforcing marginalisation and exclusion'.

The Need for General Skills

A feature of European projects based in the adult education rather than training sector has been helping long-term unemployed people to acquire or recover certain skills before they can successfuly undertake employment training.

Engelhardt (1988) stresses the importance of 'second chance' education, which includes assessment of adults' life and work experience and is integrated with training in a way which enables people to acquire basic competences. Many European projects aimed at the unemployed with fewest qualifications and skills have put stress on the acquisition of: 'key competences – core or generic problem-solving, learning techniques, information-handling, communication skills, personal effectiveness' (22). Examples are the Building on Experience programme for long-term unemployed people in Ireland which emphasises general education aspects, particularly basic processes such as helping adults to learn, set goals and be personally effective (23), and the FUNOC Project in Belgium which stresses 'social qualification' (awareness, self-help, ability to organise and change one's environment) before other training needs (24).

An English case-study has confirmed the findings of other projects in showing that the unemployed as a group are likely to be attracted by a broad range of options including practical skills-based courses, employment-related courses, group activities and courses immediately relevant to everyday life (25). According to an increasing number of people, one of the primary aims of such programmes should be to 'empower' people whose situation has induced feelings of powerlessness and helplessness, by helping them to recover a sense of control over their lives (Banks and Bryn Davies, 1990). Those involved in the REPLAN programme in England and Wales have recognised that: 'a prime purpose of provision must be not only the development of motivation and confidence but the encouragement of a sense of empowerment and ownership' (26), and an Employment Department/REPLAN publication refers to: 'evidence from all sections of adult education and training that where learners are encouraged to take control of their own learning their motivation increases and performance improves' (27).

The European experience therefore suggests that adult education programmes have as important a role to play as labour-market linked programmes in helping those most affected by unemployment to recover self-confidence and skills. The irony is that in Europe, 'adult education is everywhere ill-resourced and a poor relation of initial and employment training' (28). According to Engelhardt (1988), Sweden is the only European country where adult education has played an important role in measures to combat unemployment. He argues that a new approach to the role, content and organisational framework for adult education is now required: 'to help it combat long-term unemployment and to contribute towards developing the economy' (29).

This argument is supported by evidence suggesting that experience of adult education often stimulates a desire to undertake training. In Denmark, for instance, it has been found that participation in general education programmes plays an important part in motivating unemployed people to embark upon training, a situation which has prompted a call for schemes which 'cut right across the strongly sector-oriented adult education tradition' in that country (30).

Convergence Between Sectors

Bogard also advocates closer links between sectors to bring about 'the vital combination of general education and technical/vocational training' (31). A CEDEFOP report claims that such a convergence is rapidly developing within some EC learning systems:

> *'from a mutual recognition that only when education and training come together can we provide what might be termed an "enabling" curriculum – one which provides attractive structured learning opportunities to enable people to maximise their potential for employment throughout working life'* (32).

Many innovative adult education programmes aimed at long-term unemployed people in Europe have also entailed a reorganisation of links between employment services, local authorities, firms and social services. Bogard (1990b) reports that some Spanish schemes have closely involved municipalities; Ireland and The Netherlands have developed partnerships between adult education and local associations and charities; and (West) Germany has put stress on partnerships between adult education, employers, employment services and social services. One of the most important features of the DES REPLAN programme in England and Wales has also been its efforts to bring together the adult education services and other sectors and agencies providing educational help for the unemployed.

References

(1) See Unemployed Unit and Youthaid Working Brief, January 1991, May 1991, discussion of TEC plans for 1991-92, reported in *The Guardian*, 28 May 1991.

(2) A. Rajan and K. Walsh, 1989, 'Conclusions, implications and recommendations' in Commission of the European Communities, 1989, *Policy Measures for Combating Long-Term Unemployment in the EC since the 1984 Resolution. Social Europe Supplement*, 5/89, pp 64–65.

(3) Protests and a steady rise in unemployment have, however, stimulated plans for further measures. In June 1991, the British government announced plans to provide 15,000 new ET places; more financial help for Job Clubs and measures to assist 100,000 newly employed look for work. A 60,000-place 'Employment Action' scheme providing work experience on local projects for benefit claimants who, like ET trainees, will receive £10 on top of their benefits was also introduced.

(4) M. Oels, 1991, 'New challenges to adult education with unemployed women', in *Grassroots Education for Women in Europe*, European Bureau of Adult Education.

(5) K. L. Oglesby, 1988, *Vocational Education for Women in Western Europe: Facts, issues and future directions*, European Bureau of Adult Education, p 23. See also the same author's 'Women and education and training in Europe: issues for the 90s', *Studies in the Education of Adults*, volume 23, number 2, October 1991, pp 133–144.

(6) HMI, 1991, *Educational Responses to Unemployed Adults: Summer 1989 to Spring 1990*, Summary, para 2.

(7) See, for example, OECD, 1989, *Education and Economy in a Changing*

Society, report on an intergovernmental conference, Paris; K. O'Brien, 1990, *Adult Education: A tool for change*, report of the conference, October 1989 at Matalskolen, Denmark.

(8) Quoted by F. Jarvis, 1991, 'The market loses its image', *Education*, 5 April, p 282.

(9) Comments made by delegates at EBAE conference on women, research and education, Newbattle Abbey, May 1991 (report forthcoming).

(10) M. Howard, *The 1990s: the Skills Decade. Strategic guidance on training and enterprise*, Department of Employment.

(11) A. Tuckett, 1991, *Towards a Learning Workforce: A policy discussion paper on adult learners at work*, NIACE.

(12) A. Rajan and K. Walsh, 1989, op. cit., pp 64–65.

(13) CEDEFOP, 1990, *Summary Report on the Services Available for the Unemployed and Especially for the Long-Term Unemployed in Denmark, Federal Republic of Germany, France, Italy, the Netherlands, Portugal, Spain and the UK*, p 43.

(14) MIRE (la Mission Interministerielle Recherche Experimentation), *Evaluation des Actions d'Insertion et de Formation (AIF)*, INFO No 22, Fevrier 1991, pp 10–15.

(15) CEDEFOP, 1990, op. cit., pp 10–11.

(16) M.H. Banks and J. Bryn Davies, 1990, op. cit., S18.

(17) Ava Farringdon, address to NIACE annual study conference, April 1990.

(18) NIACE REPLAN, 1991, *Work Experience in Adult Training*, p 8.

(19) EBAE, 1988, *Adult Education and the Long-Term Unemployed*, 2, p 219.

(20) Bogard, 1990a, op. cit., pp 32–33

(21) EBAE, 1987, *Education and Training in Relation to Council of Europe Project 9*, p 68.

(22) D. R. Johnson, 1989, 'Education and training: convergence on learning for the 1990s', in CEDEFOP, *Education + Training = the Keys to the Future, Vocational Training*, 1, 1989, pp 6–8.

(23) Described in EBAE, 1988, op. cit.

(24) Described in Council of Europe, 1985, *CDCC Project No 9: The 14 pilot experiments*.

(25) FEU, 1989, *Supporting the Unemployed in Education*.

(26) NIACE REPLAN/FEU, 1990, *Drawing on Experience: REPLAN projects review*, p 9.

(27) Department of Employment/NIACE REPLAN, 1991, *New Approaches to Adult Training*.
(28) G. Bogard, 1990b, op. cit., p 23.
(29) J. Engelhardt, 1989, quoted in G. Bogard, 1990b, op. cit., p 22.
(30) CEDEFOP, 1989, *Educational and Vocational Orientation for the Adult Unemployed, in Particular the Long-Term Unemployed in Denmark*, p 47.
(31) G. Bogard, 1990b, op. cit., p 23.
(32) D. R. Johnson, 1989, op. cit.

Section 3
Effective Initiatives

Wales: Encouraging Long-term Unemployed People to Use Employment Service Options

The 'Helping Ourselves Back to Work' project was commissioned by the Department of Employment Area Office in Gwent and conducted by the People and Work Unit between December 1989 and March 1990, with funding from the Inner City Valley Initiative Programme Development Fund. The general aim was to provide a group of long-term unemployed individuals with the necessary support and encouragement to motivate them to make use of Employment Service menu options. Specific objectives were:

- to persuade participants to form a self-help group and form their own running committee
- to encourage them to reappraise their position, experience and skills
- to improve individual perceptions of the services and facilities available for the unemployed
- to improve take-up of those facilities
- to use the experiences and views of group members to inform the presentation and content of menu items and tailor them more to local needs.

A sample of 60 'hard core' unemployed individuals were selected from those not using Employment Service facilities. Most were in their 40s, had left school at the earliest opportunity and over half had no qualifications. These were invited to attend an interview on a voluntary basis. Thirty-seven people attended the first interviews, from whom an active group of 19 voluntary participants was formed.

The project's priorities were to modify the attitudes and perceptions of clients ('high level changes in behaviour require changes at the level of perception and attitude and emotional commitment to the proposed change'), and to encourage them to explore what personal changes lay within their power, with the understanding that these might involve family members and other people with whom individuals had emotional ties.

The programme comprised two initial interviews, nine sessions and a final interview. At the first interview volunteers were asked to assess themselves on a subjective well-being scale and to give details of their current activities, hopes, wants and needs; their use of employment services to date, and views on employment services provision. The second involved a review of initial comments, identification of personal objectives and concerns, agreement on areas for action and negotiation of sessions.

The sessions took the form of whole-group and small-group work involving a sharing of concerns, thoughts, developments and progress in relation to job search and other interests. Discussions were directed towards what was possible and what individuals themselves could do within the current industrial context and the range of resources available. To improve knowledge and understanding of the services available, Employment Services staff and claimant advisers were invited to join some discussions and participants visited facilities for the unemployed such as Job Clubs. The visits were followed by an evaluation of the service provided, with groups listing what they perceived as the benefits or disadvantages. The last session involved a whole-group evaluation of the project and individual presentations on how each participant would go about pursuing a particular job vacancy.

In the final interview, individuals reviewed their current activities, and job search progress, and discussed their use and perceptions of employment services since the beginning of the project, and their present hopes, needs and subjective well-being. At the end of the programme it was found that participants wished to continue, and arrangements were made for six future sessions on a regular monthly basis.

Outcomes

The project achieved its main objective, for it was found that participants at the end of the programme had dropped their 'wholly defensive stance' and displayed a demonstrably more positive attitude to the services and facilities available than they had at the start. Participants had also acquired a greater sense of purpose, improved social interaction skills and increased their self-respect. After the project, several among them started to use Employment Service options: two started to attend the local Job Club; two joined the ET programme; two were referred to literacy programmes; two used a local TAP in seeking training opportunities; and one started a job on a trial basis.

Factors Which Encouraged Recruitment and Motivation

- Written invitations to attend the initial interview at a Job Centre were in a style similar to that used in routine requests to attend RESTART interviews.
- Attendance was voluntary and welfare benefits were not affected.
- The project was characterised by a relaxed and informal person-centred approach based on trust: 'in the belief that it is only possible to begin assessing and solving problems when a good relationship has been established with individuals'.
- Travel expenses were reimbursed at an early stage during sessions: this demonstrated to people that they were there out of choice and could leave if they wished.
- The project took account of the personal situation of participants by incorporating in interviews not just the views and feelings of participants but also the views, wishes and attitudes of their partners, families and others close to them.
- The programme was designed in ways that 'stemmed from and served the self interests of clients', i.e. it was negotiated with them to reflect their wishes, interests and concerns and to give them control over their activities. A 'key principle' was to work with participants from their individual starting points towards objectives of their own choosing and at their own

pace, with stress on personal stocktaking and realistic action planning.
- Participants were offered encouragement and support in looking for the most appropriate routes to employment and 'reappraising opportunities'.
- The project brought together unemployed individuals, Employment Services staff and claimant advisers. Participants were encouraged to question and suggest potential changes to Employment Services, 'something which they had not considered possible'.

[SOURCE: People and Work Unit, 1990, 'Helping Ourselves Back to Work: Providing effective support to the long-term unemployed', Newport, Gwent.]

Bremen: A Pilot Programme for Unemployed Single Mothers Receiving Welfare Benefits

A retraining scheme has been developed in Bremen specifically for unemployed single mothers – a group with 'so many practical problems that a normal retraining programme would not work'. The scheme is divided into three phases:

- 5 months' preparation for retraining
- 24 months' retraining programme
- 6 months' support after the programme to assist women's integration into the workforce.

The initial phase helps participants to adjust to a learning situation, to brush up study skills, to identify existing experience and skills, to identify personal training needs and make decisions. The retraining programme takes place in company workshops in the service and industrial sectors and leads to a Trade and Commerce examination. During retraining, the women receive sociopedagogic support: personal counselling as well as training advice and guidance.

One of the main aims of the programme is to change participants' attitudes and expectations with regard to training and employment options. Among this target group, these relate to the problems associated with having sole responsibility for the care and upbringing of children:

> *'Factors which affect motivation and learning success with this group are the challenge and difficulties which a long training programme implies for a single mother who has no one with whom to share childcare and upbringing. This presents a dual burden for trainees – problems with childcare and feelings of guilt at not giving children undivided attention.'*

The starting premise of the programme is the belief that the commitment of single mothers to a training programme will only be achieved by a process that deals directly with their anxieties about their children and encourages them to redefine their roles and expectations. It is found that participants invariably embark on the training with the intention that no aspect of their current relationship with their children will change. In the initial phase, therefore, trainers try to modify unrealistic expectations by clarifying the differences involved in having *two* roles, those of mother and worker, and demonstrating aspects of the mothers' lives which it may be feasible to change.

> *'It was important for women during retraining to build up an image of themselves as both mother and worker, able to pursue both roles simultaneously with equal commitment. But this meant that their children also had to experience a process of change in their situation – mother's absence and her interest in her professional life. The image of the good mother who puts children before everything is replaced by a process of independence on both sides and a new qualitative concept of the time spent together.'*

As a result of this process, 'many participants are being helped to make the transition from dependence on state benefits to being an active worker'.

Factors Which Encouraged Recruitment and Retention

- The scheme employs outreach approaches and personal contacts using a language 'connected to their personal lives' to

attract women who would never approach the Employment Exchange or enrol on formal education or training schemes.
- The scheme pays the women a training allowance which is higher than their social security benefits and which is paid independently of the social security system.
- The scheme is organised and arranged in a way that takes into account the difficult situation of single parents. For example, a 'granny service' is available to look after sick children for a minimal fee during the training period.
- The scheme encourages women to redefine their roles and personal arrangements so as to encompass a view of themselves as paid workers: 'The crucial prerequisite for the successful completion of a retraining programme is this process of redefinition of the mother's role in her eyes and in her children's eyes. If this does not take place, domestic problems may mean training becomes of secondary importance and in cases of doubt will be terminated.'

[SOURCE: F. von Kuchler, 1990, 'Examples of Professional Training and Retraining Programmes for Women in West Germany', Pädagogische Arbeitsstelle des Deutschen Volkshochschul-Verbandes. See also the same writer's contribution to the volume *Grassroots Education for Women in Europe*, EBAE, 1991.]

Vosges: A Short Training Course for the Long-term Unemployed

Between 1986 and 1987, Operation 41, a pilot 80-hour training course for the long-term unemployed, was organised in Saint Die, a small town in the Vosges. The course was designed and assessed with the collaboration of the University of Nancy and was an experiment to test whether such a scheme could be adapted for use elsewhere. The primary aims of the scheme were to help individuals to be more effective in job search and acquisition, to help them change their attitudes and expectations and to consider opportunities in different sectors from those in which they had already worked. It was organised in short modules and lasted 80 hours in total. The initial stages of the course included applications to local companies, identification of local skills requirements and discussions with people in employment who had formerly been jobless about ways of making the transition back into the labour market. This was followed by specific job training.

The course attracted 45 men with few qualifications and little previous training. Few held primary school leaving certificates and even fewer held vocational training certificates.

During the course, trainers tried to encourage participants to develop a clearer vision of the kind of jobs they would apply for and to diversify their options. This did not work with all participants and it was found that some were unable to break from their occupational past and think of a new career plan. Evaluation revealed, however, that most left the course with clearer insights into what they wanted to do and clearer knowledge about the local labour market and available training and job opportunities. Participants also gained in confidence, improved their communication skills and could identify their own experience and skills. Of the 45 participants, 10 found permanent work (compared with three in an identical control group) and 16 went into further training or temporary work.

Factors Which Encouraged Recruitment and Retention

- The course was wholly local in nature: it reflected local needs and targeted local unemployed people. It brought together unemployed people and employers and generated a dialogue between the two. One of the course modules was devoted to the local environment.
- The teaching methods avoided formal instruction and used experiential techniques adapted to trainees' abilities – games, role-play and simulation – which were found to be effective in boosting communication and job search skills.
- The use of modules broke the course down into assimilable stages to be achieved at participants' own pace.

[SOURCE: ERGO, 1, Summer 1989.]

Birmingham: A Project Linking Unemployed Women and Local Employment Opportunities

In 1990, a project funded by the Community Education Development Fund in Birmingham was devised to bring unemployed women without qualifications into contact with local companies and local employment possibilities. The aim was to enable a dialogue which would help women to find out about local job options, evaluate their existing skills and experience, and broaden their expectations and aspirations.

> 'Women can only make choices when they are in a position to know what is possible within the community and what is possible within themselves. Without this broadening there is a real danger of reinforcing the limitations of their own vision and immediate aspirations.'

A secondary aim of the project was to develop a flexible, open approach that allowed women to negotiate the time, pace and direction of activities. This involved:

- initial group sessions, combining information and guidance; recording of skills and experience and relating them to work vacancies and government training schemes; discussion of the wider context of social and economic trends, attitudes to women and equal opportunities
- links with local employers and visits to workplaces (retail, manufacturing, service industries, local government) to look at work processes, recruitment, skill needs and training processes, and hold discussions with members of staff
- sessions on the accreditation of prior learning and experience and the possibilities provided by NVQs.

The project had very positive outcomes for the 16 participants. It gave women a broader perspective and enabled them to think about what they really wanted. At the end of the project, all reported increased self-esteem, greater confidence in their abilities and a more positive and decisive outlook. In addition, all were able to evaluate their unpaid skills and experience and present them in a positive way. Participation also motivated individuals to make decisions and take action. By the end of the process, some were actively seeking and gaining employment at levels appropriate to their abilities, some were seeking training or retraining courses, while others were looking for alternatives to paid employment as ways of using and enhancing their skills and getting further training. Specifically: one women started training as a youth leader; three started Home Start projects; one joined an ET programme; one enrolled on a counselling course and another on RSA and C&G courses prior to taking an OU or a polytechnic course; one woman took over an allotment and was learning about horticulture; and a group of participants initiated 'green' practices on their council estate.

For adult education staff, the project provided a valuable opportunity to be involved with the world of work in ways other than skills training:

'More can be done within existing programmes to feed in greater awareness of industry and commercial organisations as part of the development of core skills.'

It also exemplified an alternative and cost-effective way of working with women who would not have joined a formal course and who would have been intimidated by the pressures of a special training scheme:

'The "alternative-to-a course" model worked well, and more can be done to investigate the usefulness of flexible, exploratory processes. The benefits here were that the women became engaged in something that was flexible, short-term, the timing and pace of which was determined by participants. The process was integrated into the normal working package of a flexibly employed adult education worker ... By building it into existing practice, the process had more the appearance of a natural next step than of a scheme set up specially.'

Key Factors in the Scheme's Effectiveness

- The 16 participants were all recruited by personal contacts from existing community and adult education networks.

Effective Initiatives

- The process was negotiated with women to suit their time and domestic constraints and workplace visits were made possible by childcare provision. The project 'highlighted the inadequacy of formal education and training course timing for women caring for families. Few of the women would have been able to participate in full-time skills training.'
- The broad aims and open-ended nature of the project ensured that all participants made progress without feeling pressured to achieve a pre-determined outcome – a job, a qualification – and without feeling a failure if they did not.

[SOURCE: B. Bateson and G. Bateson, 1991, 'Worklink – an Adult Education, Women and Industry Project', Birmingham Education Authority.]

The Netherlands: Local Labour Market-linked Initiatives

In The Netherlands it is believed that the following elements will help the long-term unemployed improve their chances in the labour market:

- help with basic knowledge and skills
- modular courses geared to practice and based on life experience
- intensive job mediation and in-service placements.

The Centre for Vocational Training and Professional Practice (CAB) is part of the Dutch service for sheltered employment (DVW) in Enschede for unemployed people aged between 16 and 50 who have been out of work for more than 12 months. Up to 360 participants can be taken every year on an eight-week programme which involves:

- orientation to jobs available in the region
- broadening the concept of individual talents and potential through testing and training
- promotion of self-reliance

Motivating Unemployed Adults

- work experience and simulation to help restore a normal daily routine.

At the end of the eight weeks, candidates receive an evaluation report with suggestions on how to proceed with their efforts in finding suitable work or how to develop other activities including, if relevant, suggestions for further study.

Factors Which Encouraged Recruitment and Commitment

- The programme is linked to the local labour market.
- Trainees are helped to restore a daily routine and given strong support.

[SOURCE: EBAE, 1988 , 'Adult Education and the Long-Term Unemployed (1)'.]

Another scheme in The Netherlands in based on the belief that job guarantees provided in advance, linked with short, job-specific training schemes, will attract the target groups least likely to participate in training: 'It is not education the long-term unemployed are waiting for, it's a job'. Two organisations in Arnhem – Stedona (the Arnhem Educational Enterprise Foundation) and The Vocational Orientation and Training Centre (CBB) – have therefore collaborated in developing short-term training for the long-term unemployed. With ESF funding they have helped to establish an Industrial Training Centre to develop and carry out training programmes for unskilled and low-skilled unemployed, tailored to identified job profiles and industrial needs. Certificated training modules have been developed on the basis of existing demand from trade and industry, but there is also multi-skill training to offer wider development and lead to further training. The learning route designed for individuals is matched to their aspirations and skills and conceived as a ladder with rungs representing successive stages of progression: reorientation interview, orientation, employment link-up, qualification, labour market.

Effective Initiatives

The Key Factor Encouraging Recruitment

Job guarantees are clearly the key factor. The 'unique feature' of this scheme is that demand comes from industry and industry is partly responsible for the costs of training unskilled unemployed people. However, this scheme may exclude many of the most disadvantaged unemployed people, since, to gain entry to the programme, potential trainees are required to have good mental and physical health, a fixed income and good accommodation.

[SOURCE: EBAE, 1988, 'Adult Education and the Long-Term Unemployed (2)'.]

Pre-employment Training Provided by UK Employers

During the 1980s, some British employers conducted positive recruitment measures targeted at unemployed people, particularly those in the most disadvantaged groups. The strategy involved pre-employment training to offset the disadvantage unemployed people are at in the job market. Courses were, therefore, designed to help trainees through the interview process, to boost confidence and morale, to refresh basic skills and instil work habits. Two types of training were involved:

- pre-recruitment courses, generally of one to two weeks, to prepare trainees for the company's selection process (what employers are looking for, interviews, application forms, psychometric and other recruitment tests, visits to potential workplaces, etc.).
- customised training (up to 10 weeks) involving technical skills for the jobs required, work experience, social and personal skills training. The latter was usually conducted off-site by local community-based training organisations or national organisations such as Fullemploy, the Industrial Society or the Employment Department.

Recruitment to training was generally through advertisements in local newspapers, open days in companies or Job Centres. In most cases, attendance was backed up by guarantees of a job interview and, in some cases, a job for those successfully completing training. Trainees could continue to draw benefits while training, under arrangements made between employers and the local Unemployment Benefit Office and subsequently through the ET scheme.

Some Examples

Soapworks Ltd in Glasgow (a subsidiary of the Body Shop)

Soapworks was created in 1988 with a policy to recruit workers from the Easterhouse area. The company was not looking for particular skills or qualifications but for a balanced group of team workers. Some were recruited through a Training Agency work preparation course for the long-term unemployed. After interviews, 14 recruits aged between 16 and 49 were sent for a week's training to the Body Shop Training School in London. This was followed by a week at a factory where they shadowed workers doing work similar to the job they would be doing in Glasgow. Within six months, the workforce expanded to 29 and three months later to 45. According to a report:

> 'The factory's success dispels many of the myths that the long-term unemployed are demotivated and difficult to employ. We found very few long-term unemployed who did not want work. Currently there are 150 awaiting interviews and daily enquiries from others.'

William Hill

In 1989 Mecca Bookmakers developed a customised training scheme to recruit long-term unemployed individuals as trainee managers for their betting shop chain. The training involved job analysis and training modules developed and funded by Mecca, in areas such as numeracy, customer contact, health and safety and cash handling. Successful trainees were guaranteed jobs.

The trainees, mainly ethnic minority individuals, were recruited by a local community agency. Sixteen people were selected who would not meet normal selection criteria for trainee managers because disadvantaged by long-term unemployment, low educational standards, appearance, etc. They attended a 10-week course with built-in work experience at Tottenham College. The course involved regular assessment and workplace reviews. Mecca bore the costs of commissioned training modules and the remainder of the funding came from grants. Trainees were paid a government training allowance and Mecca gave a £100 bonus on completion. They were also paid travel expenses and given a week's holiday entitlement or one week's pay.

Thirteen trainees completed the course and 10 achieved the required standards. The remaining three were recruited to other Mecca posts.

TSB Birmingham

Birmingham TSB joined with Handsworth Breakthrough scheme to run a pre-recruitment training course for unemployed people, especially ethnic minority individuals, wishing to join the bank at junior clerical level (counter clerks). One of the aims was to dispel the negative image of banking and to overcome the notion that GCSEs are required for entry. No qualifications were needed for entry to what might become a long-term career, with promotion after 6 to 12 months and further opportunities for those subsequently willing to take IOB exams.

A seven-day pre-training course was run by the Industrial Society, with TSB staff giving some of the sessions. Those completing the course were guaranteed job interviews. The preliminary course used films, role-play and other exercises to coach applicants for the selection process (which would involve tests of reasoning and numeracy and a personal interview looking for qualities of leadership, initiative and teamwork). All 14 participants completed the course and seven were placed in the bank. The others were given guidance and counselling to assist them in other directions.

The BBC
1. The BBC developed a pre-recruitment course for unemployed individuals, funded by North Peckham Task Force and delivered by Fullemploy. The aims were to demonstrate the BBC's commit-

ment to equal opportunities and to draw on a pool of labour that would not normally apply for jobs in the Corporation. Ten people were recruited, mostly people without qualifications from ethnic minority groups. They attended a 13-week course which trained them in typing, word-processing and office skills. Trainees were guaranteed interviews on completion and seven were retained, while one got a job elsewhere. The course was considered very successful and several others were mounted in other parts of London.

2. The Board of Governors of the BBC Centre in Elstree has a Training Bursary scheme to train 10 long-term unemployed people a year in video-making skills. Applicants are required simply to have some interest and experience in community video work. The course is hands-on and skills-based and includes job-hunting skills. All trainees are guaranteed interviews on completion of the course. In the first two years (1985 and 1986), eight of the 20 trainees acquired TV jobs, one obtained a job in community video and six found work in related fields. In 1987 five out of 10 acquired BBC jobs, but 'the number of offers is shrinking as BBC job opportunities shrink'.

McDonalds Hamburgers Ltd
As part of a scheme funded by McDonalds and a Government Task Force, pre-recruitment training was offered to jobless people with no or few qualifications in Wolverhampton. Job interviews were guaranteed on completion. The six-week course at Bilston Community College included hygiene, new technology and literacy, as well as an Outward Bound week to encourage teamwork. Importance was placed on time-keeping, and motivating trainees through games, quizzes and prizes. Trainees were encouraged to identify with their potential employer through provision of free McDonalds meals, workplace visits and college sessions held in a 'McDonalds Room'. During the course, trainees continued to collect unemployment benefit and a special signing-on session was arranged at the college for them.

Twenty-four people aged 16 to 44 were recruited, over 50% from ethnic minority groups. All completed the course and 20 were

Effective Initiatives

hired. The others were offered other courses and alternative jobs were suggested to them. All trainees received a certificate on completion.

A second course was held in Nottingham with Nottingham Task Force. Nineteen recruits aged between 17 and 56 undertook three weeks' training and work experience. As part of the ET scheme, they continued to received benefits and a weekly £10 top-up allowance.

Copthorn Hotel, Birmingham
A pre-recruitment training course for long-term unemployed people based at the College of Food and Domestic Art received 120 applications from which 60 trainees were selected. Attendance was backed up by interview guarantees. Trainees participated in a three to four-week course primarily involving awareness training for a range of jobs, self-presentation and interview skills. About 30 completed the course, and nearly all were offered jobs. All completing trainees received a certificate.

Factors Which Encouraged Recruitment and Retention

- Commitment of the companies concerned to recruit from unemployed target groups.
- Job or interview guarantees on completion of course, offering the possibility of entry to a permanent job with, in some cases, promotion prospects.
- Use of community organisations for recruitment.
- No entry qualifications required.
- No risk to benefits.
- Travel expenses paid and in some cases bonuses and holiday pay.
- Measures to help trainees comply with DSS regulations (e.g. signing-on sessions were arranged at one college providing training).
- Certification on completion of courses.
- Schemes usually incorporated some work experience.
- Members of staff appointed to oversee recruitment and to act as liaison officers and counsellors.

- Support gained for positive action schemes from existing workforce and the unions.
- Use of local organisations and resources for training.

[SOURCE: T. Crowley-Bainton and M. White, 1990, 'Employing Unemployed People: How employers gain', Report to the Employment Service, Policy Studies Institute.]

Supportive Approaches In British Education Institutions

In the UK, where fears regarding their financial position often discourage benefit claimants from entering training or education, the provision of information, advice and support can significantly improve the recruitment and retention of unemployed individuals. Some British colleges have consequently established measures to advise and support unemployed students and help them fulfil the 'actively seeking work' obligation. At Westminster Adult Education Institute, for example, unemployed students are, at enrolment, referred to advice workers who can explain DSS regulations. Paddington College has built job search into tutorial sessions for Access and A-level courses. The college obtains a list of job vacancies and keeps records of student job applications. Students are given letters to take to Unemployment Benefit offices stating that their course of study does not exceed 21 hours and that a job search component is built in. Hammersmith and West London College also has a job search facility – a drop-in 'Job Mart' open during lunch time which offers advice, lists of job vacancies and record-keeping. The service is used mainly for advice and clarification of regulations and help with RESTART interviews.

Camden Adult Education Institute service for literacy students has developed a student record pack for those who are unemployed: this comprises a diary for keeping records of job-seeking with guidance on completing it, and slips to be completed by employers as evidence of job search Such support measures are important aids to recruitment as they:

- allay individuals' fears about losing benefits

- provide accurate information and advice to help students comply with DSS regulations, particularly the actively seeking work requirement.

[SOURCE: A. Sims and R. Pilkington, 1990, 'The Effects of Actively Seeking Work on 21-Hour Study: A practical guide to local initiatives and responses', Central and West London Open College.]

Section 4

Factors Which Encourage Participation

This brief overview of evidence from different parts of Europe makes it possible to identify some of the factors and conditions most likely to encourage unqualified unemployed people to participate in education and training. (Because of easier access to data, many of the following examples are taken from a UK context.)

People without post-school education and training experience need to be persuaded to view training and education in a more positive light. This means convincing them that there are essential differences between school and education and training for adults, that education and training can actively help them in their predicament, and that special education and training schemes will not stigmatise them or be counterproductive to their interests. National schemes sometimes fail to convey these messages:

> *'The long-term unemployed do not identify with the national image of ET projected through advertisements ... The credibility of government schemes is affected by whatever facts and half-truths are circulating' (1).*

The credibility of any education or training scheme depends on the extent to which it is seen by the target group as accessible, relevant and useful. Banks and Bryn Davies (1990) argue that any strategy to increase the motivation of unqualified unemployed people needs to: 'take into account what they themselves want, what they believe they can achieve and the kinds of risks and costs they are prepared to accommodate'. The following paragraphs suggest what schemes can do to attract more individuals from this group.

Provide Clear Information and Guidance

Lindley (1991) argues that systems of education and training should be 'transparent' as well as accessible: enabling people to know not only what opportunities are available and that they can apply, but also how to value them. This overview of research indicates the crucial importance of providing educational and vocational guidance at the beginning of unemployment rather than when a person is formally categorised as long-term unemployed:

> *'Experience has proved that the newly unemployed are much more receptive to training and more successful in gaining unemployment than those who are chronically unemployed'* (2).

> *'One lesson of the last recession is that the employability and self-confidence of the jobless declines rapidly after 12 months. Any new system has to prevent more people crossing that 12-month line and perhaps joining an underclass'* (3).

Demonstrate Clear Links Between Training/education and Employment

Most commentators make the point that long-term unemployed people want jobs, not education. However, they can be attracted to programmes which they believe will assist them in obtaining employment, particularly those which offer job guarantees or at least the guarantee of an interview on completion of training. One of the most powerful motivating strategies, therefore, is to offer training linked to jobs: 'Motivation is considerably aided by a guarantee to every trainee of at least four weeks' waged work on completion of the programme' (4).

The previous section highlights the effectiveness of schemes related to the local employment market, in particular pre-employment training to recruit unemployed people to specific sectors. However, the promises implicit in training schemes need to be realistic. The design of programmes needs to take into account both the current labour market situation and the type of jobs the target group can realistically expect. If vocational training is unrelated to these variables, it will be of little actual or perceived value.

Offer Widely Recognised Qualifications

Many practitioners have found that unqualified individuals are more likely to take education and training seriously if it leads to a nationally recognised qualification. Fuller and Saunders (1990b) argue that commitment to a training programme is determined by its perceived 'use value' (work experience) and 'exchange value' (qualifications). They suggest that education or training with low exchange value may be undervalued by the learner, whereas courses with low use value may be undervalued by employers. A study by White (1990), however, suggests that employers are more concerned with qualifications than with work experience. According to White, a survey of long-term unemployment among young adults revealed that experience and training in a previous job did not appear to improve their employment chances. This, he suggests, may be because qualifications are interpreted by employers as signs of a general aptitude or attitude whereas specific training and work experience are more difficult to evaluate because they are not standardised or comparable:

> 'During a period of unemployment, the significance of diplomas/certificates seems to increase while that of apprenticeships or work experience appears to dwindle into nothing. In programmes designed for the unemployed, the problem of recognition of the training is a crucial issue' (5).

Ensure that the Benefits of Participation Exceed the Potential Risks

Since one of the biggest barriers to participation in training or education is fear about loss or disruption of welfare benefits, an obvious incentive would be to remove that anxiety, for example by:

- providing a minimum guaranteed income level, such as has been introduced in France, the *'revenu minimum d'insertion'*. This removes unemployed people's fear of falling out of the social security safety net
- providing clear and accurate information on social security regulations and procedures. In the UK, education and training institutions can take certain measures to assist unemployed enrolees: provision of a letter of declaration detailing the nature of the course, the number of contact hours and type of certification, and confirming that the student will be available immediately if a vacancy or interview occurs
- nominating a staff member as a link person to co-ordinate advice and information to students taking advantage of the 21-hour rule; to provide advice and guidance; to maintain links with the DSS, benefit offices and employment services and to be the named contact if a student is required for an interview
- providing, at enrolment, written information for students, giving details of the operation of the 21-hour rule, suitable courses and names of link persons
- maintaining a register of students studying under the concession
- providing comprehensive job search facilities within the institution
- establishing a referral system so that students can be referred to a source of expert advice and representation (e.g. CAB, Law Centre)
- liaising with RESTART counsellors/teams to ensure that they are aware of the extent and nature of courses available to the unemployed (6).

Offer Financial Incentives to Those Who Undertake Education/training

There is clear evidence that financial incentives are a powerful motivating factor and that unemployed people are likely to be attracted to training which offers allowances greater than welfare benefits.

> 'The correct financial incentive is a necessary prerequisite that needs to be present before the impact of other enabling conditions can take full effect' (7).

> 'Forget the other things. Pay is the motivator; pay them right and there's no problem' (Education and Training Manager, IMS).

Evidence from the UK also suggests that training allowances which are paid independently of social security benefits have a more positive effect on people's motivation than top-ups to welfare benefits:

> 'There is an important psychological benefit of having a training allowance rather than benefit. A training allowance gives people a different relationship with the world. ET is just a continuation of benefit and people may not come just because of that' (Tutor with unemployed, Bristol).

Other types of financial incentives to undertake training or education are:

Fee remission: In the UK this has been an effective means of attracting many unemployed students to colleges. For example, when Richmond Adult and Community College introduced vouchers allowing unemployed students to enrol on a number of part-time courses, a high proportion of new students were people who had left school at the earliest opportunity (NIACE REPLAN, 1988).

Training credits: Vouchers which can be exchanged for training provided by employers or other training providers have been introduced in Bremen. There, job seekers can draw one training voucher per half-year from the regional Employment Office, together with a list of institutions and programmes. There is no qualifying period and the sole condition for eligibility is to be registered with the Office. In England and Wales, training credit schemes entitling young people to education and training to approved standards are currently being piloted and the system is to be extended. There have been calls for the scheme to be extended to adults, the unemployed in particular. In 1991 a pilot scheme involving guidance and counselling vouchers for the unemployed was introduced.

Personal income tax allowances: A system of tax allowances for those paying for their own education or training has been announced in England and Wales, although this may not help those in a precarious financial situation.

Loans: Career development loans for employment-related training is currently open to anyone 18 or over, in or out of work, who lives or intends to work in Great Britain. However, many unemployed people will be unwilling to take on additional debts unless the training offers the guarantee of a job.

Use Targeted Outreach Approaches

Those in non-participant categories are not easily persuaded to undertake education or training by advertising or other forms of publicity. A common finding of the education projects discussed in Council of Europe Project 9 (Council of Europe, 1985) was that it required a far more extensive and intensive outreach process than expected to overcome negative reactions such as apathy, indifference, suspicion and hostility, and to convince long-term unemployed people that they could be helped.

Research consistently shows that individuals do not wish to engage in activities that are not perceived as normal within their peer and reference groups, and one of the most effective recruitment strategies has been identified as group targeting using local organisations and networks. Crowley-Bainton and White (1990) report that schemes targeted at long-term unemployed people can be most effectively 'sold' to them by persuading community organisations with credibility in the area to promote the scheme among their members.

Group acceptance of a scheme can also be achieved by identifying 'opinion leaders' in a group and persuading them of the merits of a programme (Larson, 1980) or by harnessing the goodwill of existing students in recruitment efforts. At Hinckley College, unemployed students do their own marketing. They have a desk at the local Job Centre and attend the DSS every day on a rota basis. In Consett, it was observed that the reassurances of other students were crucial to redundant steelworkers' decisions to enrol in education and training programmes (FEU, 1985).

Recognise Personal Circumstances

Family Ties and Responsibilities

Unemployment affects not just individuals but their families and communities, yet most schemes address the unemployed as if they alone were affected. Initiatives which take into account, in their organisation and content, the overall situation of the unemployed person – as a spouse, as a parent, as a carer for other adults – are more likely to succeed than others. One scheme which attempted to address unemployment in terms of its effects on the family was a pilot residential programme offered in Bremen to long-term unemployed individuals and their families. The theme was family life and the general aims were to increase understanding that unemployment is not a personal failure and to work out a personal 'reactivation strategy' with individuals and their families.

Most reports comment on the need for good childcare arrangements to enable unemployed women to participate in training or education schemes. However, few schemes have used as their starting point the issue that most affects and hinders mothers' participation: their anxieties about their children.

Location

A precondition of successful adult learning, that learning arrangements should fit adults' personal situation and needs, is especially necessary in the case of the unemployed. Prolonged unemployment leads to increasing isolation and insecurity. For psychological as well as financial reasons, many unemployed people do not wish to travel outside a two-mile radius. For this reason some British education centres and colleges have successfully sited education and training programmes for the adult unemployed in informal community locations. It has also been found that venues which are physically separated from the formal educational environment are often necessary to overcome initial resistance by those who left school at the minimum leaving age (FEU, 1986).

Respond to Individual Learning Needs

Unqualified people with no post-school education or training are at a strong disadvantage in formal education or training schemes if they are not offered programmes which remedy major handicaps such as lack of basic skills, language skills and learning skills; which take stock of existing knowledge and skills; and which 'restore self-confidence, develop initiative and allow individuals to recover motivation at their own pace' (8). This is especially true for women, many of whom require women-only preparatory programmes to help them recognise and evaluate their skills and experience and regain the confidence to join a formal education or training programme.

Provide Counselling Support

Many long-term unemployed individuals experience financial difficulties and family stress which affects their ability to complete a programme. At one college, for example, tutors on the unemployed programme have received anxious phone calls late at night: 'We need a trained counsellor and a social services worker at the end of the phone' (9). Banks and Bryn Davies (1990) argue that skilled psychological intervention is required to support and guide unemployed participants through difficult stages, and that REST-ART and other Employment Services staff need more training and support than they currently receive. Project workers in Wales (People and Work Unit, 1990) also stress the importance, in preliminary interviews, of counselling not just individuals but also their partners and others close to them. They recommend that Employment Services staff with the responsibility of referring clients to special schemes be trained in counselling skills, with particular emphasis on interpersonal aspects – understanding the impact of unemployment on individuals and their families – and that clients be allocated to counsellors/advisers on a case-load basis, with the frequency of interview related to individual need.

Encourage Group Support

Since social isolation is a key factor in unemployment, one of the benefits of participation is meeting other adults. A study of unemployed adults in further education (FEU, 1989) found that over 86% particularly enjoyed meeting others and for RESTART students this was a significant factor. Group work appears to be a key factor in student support and retention.

Provide Practical Work Experience and Help With Establishment of Work Routine

This condition can only be achieved if employers are willing to take on the least qualified and skilled unemployed as trainees.

Encourge Employers to Take on Unemployed Trainees

Pre-employment training has been described as an extremely useful and versatile tool to ease people out of unemployment and back into jobs, particularly when it offers job or interview guarantees (Crowley-Bainton and White, 1990). However, the evidence suggests that individuals in the most disadvantaged unemployed categories are often excluded from training placements. It may require special incentives to persuade employers to offer training placements to these groups, such as higher wage subsidies or temporary waiving of employer insurance contributions. In the 1980s, France introduced employment contracts enabling long-term unemployed people aged over 26 to be taken on for a minimum of two years by an employer, during which time they were entitled to receive training lasting at least 600 hours. Employees' wages were covered by the scheme, and at the end of the two years, employers were encouraged to retain them full-time in return for a year-long exemption from paying their Social Security contributions (10).

In England and Wales, there is some official recognition of the advantages of recruiting staff who are available for work rather than those who have to be tempted away from other jobs:

> 'By recruiting from groups who are at a disadvantage in the job market – because they have been out of jobs for a while or because they have disabilities, language or learning difficulties – you create a strong loyalty bond. Motivation for work is often stronger amongst people who have had to overcome such disadvantages' (11).

There is evidence that positive measures by employers to recruit unemployed and otherwise disadvantaged groups can be beneficial to both parties. An evaluation of targeted pre-employment training schemes, including those outlined in the previous section, lists the benefits to companies as:

Easing staff shortages: Those experiencing recruitment or retention problems, particularly for lower-paid jobs, were tapping new pools of labour not reached by other methods of recruitment.

Cost-effectiveness: The sample of employers studied found that the costs of providing pre-employment training were not high compared with the costs of advertising.

Encouraging staff commitment and retention: The companies concerned found that pre-employment courses encouraged a strong commitment to the company and led to staff retention.

Improving local community relations: In many cases, targeted pre-training was found to improve relations with the local community and increase interest in working for the company.

Improving job analysis procedures: In designing customised training programmes for unemployed groups, some companies had, for the first time, conducted thorough job analyses and prepared structured training modules. These were subsequently found valuable for general recruitment purposes (12).

References

(1) M. H. Banks and J. Bryn Davies, 1990, op. cit., S17.
(2) Association of Canadian Community Colleges, 1986, *Practical Experiences with the Canadian Jobs Strategy*, quoted by R. Edwards, 'Guidance and unemployment in Canada', *Adults Learning*, volume 2, number 10, June 1991.
(3) C. Weston, 'Long-term jobless need more than dole', *The Guardian*, 4 May, 1991.
(4) NIACE REPLAN, 1991, op. cit., p 13.
(5) M. White, 'Information et chômage des jeunes', *Sociologie du Travail*, 4, 1990, pp 529–541 (author's translation)
(6) NIACE REPLAN, 1990, *The '21 Hour Rule' and Support for Adult Learners*.
(7) M.H. Banks and J. Bryn Davies, 1990, op. cit., S15, p 2.
(8) G. Bogard, 1990a, op. cit., pp 32–33.
(9) A. Farringdon, address to NIACE annual study conference, April 1990.
(10) European Documents 2, Social Europe Supplement 5/89, Chapter 6.
(11) Employment Department, 1991, *The Business of Success: TECs unlock potential*, pp 26–27.
(12) T. Crowley-Bainton and M. White, 1990, op. cit., pp 1–17.

Section 5

Conclusions

This overview of research and practice in Britain and other parts of Europe makes clear that it is not possible to consider the motivation of individuals with few qualifications or skills in isolation from:

The economic context: The current state of the labour market.

The social context: The experience, attitudes and expectations of different socio-economic groups.

The educational context: The extent and nature of available options and the criteria governing access to them.

The Economic Context

The typical programme model for the long-term unemployed in Europe and other parts of the Western world involves wage subsidies to assist employers to provide work experience and training. But there is little evidence that, as currently operated, such schemes assist trainees in gaining lasting employment. White (1990) has found that training-cum-placement schemes for young long-term unemployed adults actually reduce rather than enhance their employment chances. There is also a danger that such schemes might be abused by employers:

'The idea is that the temporary subsidy of training and work experience will result in the unemployed person being maintained in employment after the programme comes to an end. The danger is, of course, that the programme becomes a revolving door with employers maintaining a continuous flow of subsidised labour at

> *the expense of individuals and the taxpayer. There is no guarantee for participants in the programmes that they will receive a job as a result of their participation. Job substitution is also a possibility'* (1).

The failure of national training schemes to help a significant number of the least qualified and skilled unemployed back into permanent employment may be due in part to a lack of connection between such schemes and the current state of the labour market. Lindley (1991) refers to a virtuous circle linking expectation, attainment and motivation which cannot be seen in isolation from the labour market. Dwindling job opportunities clearly reinforce reluctance to attend training schemes, and the indications are that it is becoming increasingly difficult to persuade employers to select recruits from the long-term unemployed and to offer work placements to trainees, although some positive pre-training initiatives have demonstrated the benefits to firms of looking beyond their traditional pools of labour. However, without greater incentives employers are unlikely to change their recruitment practices, particularly at a time of recession:

> *'The base-line is that unemployment is not their concern. In seeking personnel they are concerned with day-to-day, leading-edge issues rather than long-term issues'* (2).

The tendency to separate the vocational debate from the state of the labour market means that the question of what jobs unskilled groups can realistically hope for or expect after training is not adequately addressed. The unpromising results of the Employment Training model prompt the question whether it is realistic (or fair) to offer long-term unemployed people training, with the implication that this will improve their employment prospects, when the only jobs available to them will be temporary, insecure and low-paid. Church (1987) has interpreted the repeated demand for 'flexibility and adaptability' in the labour force as a demand for low-skilled labour, while others have expressed scepticism about claims that skills in new technology are vital to securing employment:

> *'We are told over and over again that the jobs of the future will*

demand highly qualified people. But ... the evidence is that the overwhelming majority [of new areas of employment] will be found in labour-intensive industries which are not so much low-tech as no-tech. The evidence on technical change is that it has resulted in operatives having next to no skill ... because modern industry requires so little of its operatives. This, not low ability, is the reason for low levels of skills' (3).

These arguments reinforce the case against too strong an emphasis on narrow vocational training schemes, particularly in areas of very high unemployment, except where such schemes are backed up by job or interview guarantees within specific employment sectors.

The Social Context

The unqualified and low-skilled unemployed are one of several segments of the adult population who, for a variety of reasons, do not voluntarily engage in educational activity. However, their reluctance is compounded by the negative effects of unemployment, particularly the gradual demoralisation and lack of self-esteem that prolonged joblessness brings. In the search for adequate solutions to this, it is necessary to look beyond the motivation of individuals. In many Western societies, adult education and training, though ostensibly open to all, chiefly benefit a small, more advantaged segment of the population. Wider participation will require a fundamental change in societal attitudes:

'Learning has to become socially acceptable and a source of self-esteem if the vicious circle of low standards of education and training, leading to low skills and knowledge, low profits and low investment, is to be broken' (4).

It is widely recognised by adult educators in Europe that although education and training have an important role to play in offering those most affected by unemployment new options and possibilities, they cannot significantly alter the position of unqualified and low-skilled groups so long as unemployment reflects prevailing social structures and divisions:

> *'Something has to be done about the social processes and mechanisms which lead to the risk of unemployment and social exclusion. If the segmentation of the labour market is based on social divisions, how can training change this process? How can training counterbalance the effects of other processes which produce, encourage or destabilise social divisions?'* (5).

The Educational Context

One of the most significant findings of the present study is that some national training schemes for the long-term unemployed actually reflect and reinforce the processes that lead to unemployment. Some of the factors mentioned in Section 2 – insufficient training places; selective entry procedures which screen out those with disadvantages or additional learning needs; bureaucratic procedures regarding part-time study and benefit entitlement; lack of adequate counselling and guidance to explain available options and individual benefit positions – effectively impose a double exclusion on the individuals already excluded from employment and most vulnerable to long-term unemployment: people with no qualifications and skills and those with additional disadvantages to do with age, race, special learning needs, physical or mental handicap (6). Although training has helped many unemployed individuals, it has made little impact on the overall disadvantaged position of these particular groups. The view that certain groups of unemployed lack the motivation to attend training to improve their employment chances cannot be sustained so long as national training schemes operate discriminatory entry procedures. Thus any exploration of unemployed people's motivation to undertake training and education needs to be balanced by consideration of the measures taken to promote and provide training and education for them:

> *'(It) is not only a matter of motivation and personal training but also a question of the will and mobilisation of all the partners*

Conclusions

concerned – *administrators, professionals, voluntary bodies, politicians, etc.* – *who, each at their own level, can pursue concerted efforts to find solutions*' (7).

In short, any exploration of unemployed people's motivation to undertake training cannot be separated from consideration of the readiness and capacity of policy-makers, employers and education and training providers to resource, design and deliver accessible, attractive and worthwhile learning options for them.

The Implications for Education and Training Policy

In view of the diversity of cultures, national economies and education/training systems, not to mention the diversity of unemployed individuals themselves, no definitive strategy or programme model can be proposed to help unqualified groups in Europe to improve their employment prospects. However, the available research indicates that unqualified and low-skilled individuals are most likely to be recruited to education and training if certain conditions are met; notably when:

- there are seen to be solid benefits or 'pay-offs'
- participation presents no threat to a precarious financial situation
- learning arrangements and conditions fit in with personal circumstances and do not disrupt family living patterns
- schemes respond to individual learning characteristics and requirements and provide help in areas such as basic skills, language needs, general learning skills, lack of self-confidence.

The first of these conditions is the essential pre-requisite of any scheme, since no one will voluntarily attend a scheme if there are no apparent benefits to be gained. However, no strategy to persuade unemployed people to participate will succeed if it does not take account of the other three conditions, all of which relate to the personal situation and needs of an individual. Research and reports of schemes highlight the importance, in recruitment approaches, of seeing unemployed people not as individuals without ties, but as part of a family or larger social and economic unit. This means improving the interface between employment services and unemployed people, with attention to the style of preliminary contacts and stress on sensitive guidance and counselling. It also means that targeted education or training programmes, their content, presentation and organisation, should take into account the whole person, not just their employment potential.

There are a number of diverging views on the forms education or training schemes for the unemployed should take. White (1990) argues that special schemes stigmatise individuals as unemployable and recommends that unemployed people be offered education and training in forms indistinguishable from those offered to people in work. Lindley (1991) advocates a national training system for the unemployed which is geared to the achievement of agreed standards, with four objectives – certification, flexibility, access and acceptability. But to provide such a scheme would require an initial investment by government which, he argues, should move towards providing a minimum commitment of Vocational Education and Training (VET) funding for each individual:

'The nettle of direct financial support of individuals needs to be grasped more firmly if adult commitment to VET is to be harnessed effectively' (8).

Other analysts believe that European governments should subsidise broader education/training programmes for less qualified and skilled unemployed groups rather than, as at present, prioritising only the kind of training considered economically useful. This view is given weight by evidence from areas of high unemployment (FEU, 1985) that it can be unrealistic to expect people with limited work experience to enter a training scheme with a clear set of instrumental objectives. Some of the schemes outlined in Section 3 indicate that it is more effective to offer programmes which aim to help people explore a number of options and which encourage greater self-reliance. However, in Britain at least:

'Education is being asked to look for ways of working which

increase people's control over their life choices, whilst, increasingly, it is being constrained by narrowness of purpose' (9).

This is not an argument against occupational training but an argument for schemes which, in addition to developing work skills, improve general and transferable skills and recognise the broader aims of education. Engelhardt (1988) advocates a mix of education, training and counselling measures involving an informal approach, individual experience and social activities, with an emphasis on social interaction and construction of social relationships to help students help themselves and recover self-confidence. This kind of approach calls for the convergence of training and adult education systems and increased collaboration between the different agencies involved in assisting the unemployed. It is widely recognised that one of the most valuable features of the Department of Education and Science REPLAN programme in England and Wales has been its stress on collaboration between different agencies in offering improved opportunities to the adult unemployed, raising awareness of the obstacles confronting individuals wishing to undertake education or training, and promoting strategies for change. Such collaboration is now happening increasingly on a European level. For example, a database of 1,700 local projects for the long-term unemployed has recently been established by ERGO, the European Community Action Programme for jobless people, to enable policy-makers and education and training practitioners to exchange information, experience and views. This short REPLAN project, which has brought together some of the insights and experience from work with the unemployed in Europe, suggests that international collaboration of this kind can be of immense value in exploring ways of providing useful and creative options for those most disadvantaged in the labour market.

References

(1) R. Edwards, 1991, op. cit.
(2) Susan Wood, Education and Training Manager, Institute of Personnel management, in conversation with the author.
(3) F. Webster and K. Robins, 'The reality behind the rhetoric', *The Guardian*, 17 December 1987, quoted in L. Saunders, 1989, op. cit., p 96.
(4) Sir Christopher Ball, quoted by F. Jarvis, 1991, op. cit.
(5) G. Bogard, 1990a, op. cit., p 30.
(6) In spring 1991, the Training and Enterprise Councils warned that, on current funding levels, they could not guarantee a place for every adult out of work for more than six months or cater for disadvantaged groups with particular learning needs. (Reported in *The Guardian*, 28 May 1991.)
(7) EBAE, 1988, *The Place of General and Liberal Education in Special Programmes for the Long-Term Unemployed*, p 30.
(8) R.M. Lindley, 1991, op. cit., p 220.
(9) B. and G. Bateson, 1991, op. cit., p 10.

Bibliography

Ball, Sir Christopher, 1991, *Learning Pays: The role of post-compulsory education and training*, Interim Report, April 1991, Royal Society of Arts/Industry Matters.

Banks, M.H. and Bryn Davies, J., 1990, *Motivation, Unemployment and Employment Department Programmes*, Research Paper 80, MRC/ESRC Social and Applied Psychology Unit, Department of Psychology, University of Sheffield.

Bogard, G., 1990a, *Adult Education and Social Change*, Interim Report 1989–1990, Council for Cultural Co-operation, Strasbourg.

— 1990b, *Adult Education and Social Change: The long-term unemployed*, 1989 Consolidated Progress Report, Council for Cultural Co-operation, Strasbourg.

CEDEFOP, 1989, *Educational and Vocational Orientation for the Adult Unemployed, in Particular the Long-Term Unemployed in Denmark*, Berlin.

— 1989, 'Education + Training = the keys to the future', *Vocational Training*, number 1 1989, pp 6–8.

— 1990, *Vocational Guidance and Counselling for Adults*, abridged version of summary report of services for unemployed and particularly long-term unemployed in Denmark, Federal Republic of Germany, France, Italy, Portugal, Spain and the UK.

Church, A., 1987, 'Inner city decline and regeneration', in P. Brown and D.N. Ashton (eds), 1987, *Redundancy, Unemployment and Labour Markets*, Falmer Press.

Commission of the European Communities, 1989, *Policy Measures for Combating Long-term Unemployment in the EC since the 1984 Resolution*, Social Europe, Supplement 5/89.

Council for Cultural Co-operation, 1986, *Responses to Unemployment and the Consequences of Economic Restructuring*, CDCC Project No 9, Chislehurst Seminar, July 1985.

Council of Europe, 1985, *CDCC Project No 9: The 14 pilot experiments*, Strasbourg.

Crowley-Bainton, T. and White, M., 1990, *Employing Unemployed People:*

How employers gain, Report to the Employment Service by the Policy Studies Institute.

The Danish Federation of Unions, Ministry of Cultural Affairs and Danish Research and Development Centre for Adult Education, 1990, *Adult Education: A tool for change*, Report of a conference held in October 1989 in Metalskolen, Jorlunde, Denmark.

de Montlibert, C., 1973, 'Le public de la formation des adultes', *Revue Française Sociologique*, XIV, pp 529–545.

Department of Employment, 1988, *Training for Employment*.
— 1990, *1990s: The Skills Decade: strategic guidance on training and enterprise*.
— 1991, *The Business of Success: TECs unlock potential*.

Department of Employment/NIACE REPLAN, 1991, *New Approaches to Adult Training*.

Edwards, R., 1991, 'Guidance and unemployment in Canada', *Adults Learning*, volume 2, number 10, June 1991.

Engelhardt, J., 1988, *Education des Adultes et Mutations Sociales. Etude préliminaire sur l'education des adultes chômeurs de longue durée: relations entre l'apprentissage et le travail*, Conseil de la Co-operation Culturelle, Council of Europe, Strasbourg.

European Bureau of Adult Education, 1987, *Education and Training in Relation to Council of Europe Project 9*.
— 1988a, *Adult Education and the Long-term Unemployed, 1*.
— 1988b, *Adult Education and the Long-term Unemployed, 2*.

Fuller, A. and Saunders, M., 1990a, *The Potential Take-Up of Mass Training*, Institute for Research and Development in Post-Compulsory Education, Lancaster University.
— 1990b, *The Paradox of Open Learning at Work*, The Association for Education and Training Technology International Conference, April 1990.

Further Education Unit, 1985, *Consett: A case study of education and unemployment*.
— 1986, *Retraining Adults*.
— 1989, *Supporting the Unemployed in Further Education: Stockton-Billingham Technical College*.

Gooderham, P.H., 1987, 'Reference group theory and adult education', *Adult Education Quarterly*, volume 37, number 3, pp 140–151.

Greenhalgh, G. and Stewart, M., 1987, 'The effects and determinants of training', *Oxford Bulletin of Economics and Statistics*, volume 49, number 2, pp 171–190.

Hedoux, J., 1981, 'Les non-publics de la formation collective', *Education Permanente*, number 61, pp 89–105.

Institute of Personnel Management, 1990, *A National Development Agenda: Creating a national strategy for education, training and people development*.

Larson, G.A., 1980, 'Overcoming barriers to communication', *New Directions for Continuing Education*, volume 8, number 18.

Lindley, R.M., 1991, 'Individuals, human resources and markets', in J. Stevens and R. Mackay (eds), *Training and Competetiveness*, NEDO Policy Issues Series, Kogan Page.

McCorry, M., 1989, *Women and the Need for Training*, Women's Education Project, Belfast.

McGivney, V., 1990, *Education's for Other People: Access to education for non-participant adults*, NIACE.

Munn, P. and MacDonald, C., 1988, *Adult Participation in Education and Training*, SCRE Publication 100.

NIACE REPLAN, 1988, *Educational Vouchers for Unemployed Adults*.
— 1989, *Educational Guidance for Unemployed Adults*.
— 1990, *The 21 Hour Rule and Support for Adult Learners*.

NIACE REPLAN/FEU, 1990, *Drawing on Experience: REPLAN projects review*.

OECD, 1989, *Education and Economy in a Changing Society*, report on an intergovernmental conference, OECD, Paris.

Oglesby, K.L., 1988, *Vocational Education for Women in Western Europe: Facts, issues and future directions*, European Bureau of Adult Education.

Payne, J., 1990, *Adult off-the-job Skills Training: An evaluation study*, Policy Studies Institute.

People and Work Unit, 1987, *The Older Long-Term Unemployed*, Newport, Gwent.
— 1990, *Helping Ourselves Back to Work: Providing effective support to the long-term unemployed*, Final Report, Newport, Gwent.

Raffe, D. and Smith, P., 1987, 'Young people's attitudes to YTS: the first two years', *British Educational Research Journal*, volume 13, number 3, pp 241–260.

Saunders, L. 1989, *Training and Development: An evaluation of Docklands Skillnet Quick Start Initiatives*, FEU/REPLAN.

Training Agency, 1989, *Training in Britain: A study of funding, activities and attitudes*.

Tuckett, A., 1991, *Towards a Learning Workforce: A policy discussion paper on adult learners at work*, NIACE.

White, M., 1989, 'Motivating education and training', *Policy Studies*, volume 10, number 1, pp 29–40.

— 1990, 'Information et chômage des jeunes', *Sociologie du Travail*, number 4, 1990, pp 529–541.

Woodley A., *et al.*, 1987, *Choosing to Learn: Adults in education*, SRHE/Open University Press.